*How Cycling
Can Save the World*

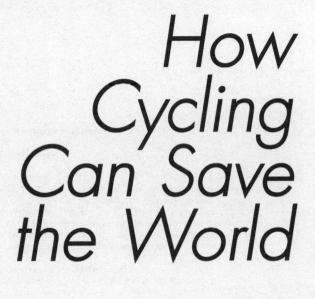

How Cycling Can Save the World

Peter Walker

A TarcherPerigee Book

For Shelly

tarcherperigee

An imprint of Penguin Random House LLC
375 Hudson Street
New York, New York 10014

Tarcher and Perigee are registered trademarks, and the colophon is a trademark of Penguin Random House LLC.

Most TarcherPerigee books are available at special quantity discounts for bulk purchase for sales promotions, premiums, fund-raising, and educational needs. Special books or book excerpts also can be created to fit specific needs. For details, write: SpecialMarkets@penguinrandomhouse.com.

ISBN 9780143111771

Printed in the United States of America
1   2   3   4   5   6   7   8   9   10

Book design by Elke Sigal

CONTENTS

Not Everyone on a Bike Is a Cyclist

It was about ten thirty on a sunny Sunday morning, a couple of days before I sat down to write this, when the flotilla of cyclists came into view from around a corner. There must have been about thirty of them, riding more or less *every* sort of bike you could imagine. At the front, pedaling an ancient folding machine at a sedate, regal cadence, was a woman probably in her sixties, wearing red trousers and a bright blue visor to shield her eyes from the glare. As I watched from the pavement she gave me a grin in passing.

Behind her were men and women of various ages, a few dressed up in the default city cycling garb of luminous jacket and shiny helmet, but most in ordinary clothes, on very everyday bikes. I had no idea if they were some sort of unfathomable organized group, or whether the arbitrary actions of traffic lights and chance had somehow coalesced them into this wonderful, accidental peloton.

But then thought struck me: either way, these people wouldn't have been here just a few months ago.

This was a road in central London called Lower Thames Street, which, as its name suggests, adjoins the river that flows through the city. An ancient thoroughfare—it was mentioned in the city's eleventh-century customs records—the road was widened and rebuilt in the 1960s, turned into the sort of double-lane urban freeway so popular in that era, when the dominance of the car appeared absolute and forever.

After the road was rebuilt for cars, very few cyclists would ride on it. It tended to be only the gung ho and bold who did so, almost all young men, often professional cycle messengers in a hurry, those who didn't mind holding a lane amid a stream of taxis and trucks, speeding under the bridges and along the concrete canyons. I was always a reasonably confident rider, but I'd try to avoid Lower Thames Street if I could. It just wasn't fun. The idea of a woman in her sixties choosing to cycle along it, even on a Sunday morning, would have been absurd. Such cyclists were excluded from large sections of their city.

So what changed? It was nothing more than a bike lane. In 2014, Lower Thames Street was selected as part of the route for one of London's first two modern, Dutch-style routes, boldly called Cycle Superhighways, which would protect riders from the motor traffic with continuous curbs, protected junctions, and bike-only traffic light sequences.

This was a controversial process. Businesses along the

way objected, saying the lanes would bring London to a halt. The trade group representing the city's iconic black cabs openly laughed at the idea that there were enough riders around to fill such broad bike thoroughfares. Outside of rush hour they would be unused, it predicted—a failure, a tumbleweed-strewn embarrassment.

In May 2015, the lanes opened, one running north to south and a longer route, taking in Lower Thames Street, heading east to west. And then the cyclists arrived. In a mass. My regular ride to work sees me ride along the north–south superhighway. I had begun cycling in London two decades before, when to do so made you something of a freak, an exception. At the time, other riders were so sufficiently rare that you'd sometimes nod in acknowledgment as you passed. Now, on the new, separated lane, I regularly wait at traffic lights amid a massed pack of two dozen or more cyclists.

For me, more interesting even than the numbers is the identity of some of these new riders. London's bike culture has long been dominated by speedy young men riding rapid bikes in specialized clothing, a product of the feral traffic culture and lack of dedicated provision for cyclists. But now other people are emerging on bikes: older, younger, slower, dressed in ordinary clothes, not riding lightweight racing bikes with ultraskinny tires.

This book is ultimately about everyday riders, and the astonishing and varied ways in which they can transform the urban environment and way of living for the better. It's about people like the sixtysomething woman with the visor and her motley gang of fellow riders.

In fact, you could even say this book isn't about cyclists at all. In one sense it is, of course. It describes the many wonderful and unexpected ways that lives and societies can improve if only more people decide they are happy to ride a bike. And if you ride a bike, you're cycling, and thus a cyclist. Correct?

Well, yes and no. In many places, particularly the UK, America, Australia, or anywhere else that the private car still dominates, if you tell someone, *I'm a cyclist*, they're likely to make a few instant assumptions. You're an enthusiast. An advocate, even. You ride everywhere, and make a vocal point of doing so. You might have opinions about gear ratios and a drawer full of garish, figure-hugging bike clothes.

I partly fall into that category. I have cycled regularly, and occasionally for long distances, for about twenty years. While I'm a news journalist I've also written quite a bit about cycling issues for my newspaper, *The Guardian*. I receive occasional bike-themed Christmas presents.

But I think the world needs fewer people like me, or perhaps more accurately it needs more bike riders like the crowd on Lower Thames Street, who treat cycling a whole lot less seriously. If cycling is indeed going to save the world, it won't be the Lycra-clad road warriors who'll be doing it. The big changes— and they can be huge—happen when a nation doesn't see cycling as a hobby, a sport, a mission, let alone a way of life. They happen when it becomes nothing more than a convenient, quick, cheap way of getting about, with the unintended bonus being the fact that you get some exercise in the process.

This is, sadly, not very common in the more car-centered nations. Cyclists are still generally viewed as a breed, a niche. They are also seen as a curiously homogenous mass. The moment I swing my legs over a crossbar, it appears, I'm a blob within a group. It doesn't matter that I also use cars, trains, buses, the Underground, my own two feet, occasionally taxis or planes, very occasionally trams, and very, very rarely the slightly eccentric and little-used cable car link over the River Thames in East London. For some reason it's only a bike that defines me.

Things are very different elsewhere. The Dutch and Danish—you'll be hearing a fair bit more about them in this book—tend to view cycling as little more than a particularly efficient form of walking. In such countries, bike riding is so ubiquitous, so normal, that almost no one defines themselves as a cyclist, any more than they might, say, define themselves as a wearer of coats or a person who takes showers.

For myself, as the years go on, while I still occasionally gaze longingly at shiny, expensive bikes in magazines, more of my actual cycling is along this continental European model. I now mainly ride clad in ordinary clothes on a solid, upright bike with a basket at the front and child seat (and sometimes a child) at the back. I make short trips to the shops, or work, or to a school. Gradually and gratifyingly, it seems, I'm becoming part of the solution.

This is important because the overwhelming evidence is that mass cycling, the sort where, say, 20 percent or even 30 percent of all trips in a country are made by bike, only happens when cycling becomes mainstream. That might seem self-evident, but it can't be stressed too much. This means you will never get very many people cycling when the bulk of riders are kitted out with helmets, Day-Glo jackets, helmet-mounted video cameras, and all the other high-tech accoutrements seen in less-bike-friendly nations. Cycling, dressed up as a hobby, let alone an extreme sport, will never attract more than a few percent of people to take part.

I delve into the mysterious and counterintuitive world of helmets and high-visibility gear later in the book. But it's worth immediately noting this: while they're not inherently bad, they're less a safety device for cycling than a symptom of a road network where no cyclist can truly feel safe.

So what is the answer? That leads us to the other big point. As Lower Thames Street (and countless other places) show, mass cycling needs decent infrastructure and planning. Everywhere with such cycling has a few things in common: notably, segregated lanes that shield riders with a physical barrier on busy roads, and lower traffic speeds on smaller routes. As soon as this happens, the bike helmets and fluorescent waistcoats suddenly disappear. They're not needed anymore.

Such systems need to be not just well designed and maintained but also cohesive, connected, and able to protect riders at perilous points like junctions. They must be secure and navigable for cyclists of all speeds and confidence, including children and older people. They need planning, investment, and above all the political will to take space from motor vehicles—elements that can be all too rare.

One question remains, that which frames this book: *Why?* Why should car drivers, still the majority transport users in virtually all industrialized countries, make way for these anachronistic, bumbling, bell-tinkling, grease-trousered, wicker-basketed, two-wheeled interlopers?

I seek to explain all this in the coming chapters, but for now let's quickly imagine what would happen if I could press a magic button and transform my own country's derisory 2 percent or so statistic for the share of all journeys that are made using a bike[1] to a near-Dutch level of around 25 percent.[2]

In an instant it would mean that many millions of people in a chronically sedentary nation would make a large number of physically active journeys a year. I detail the ongoing public health disaster from inactivity in the first chapter, but even cautious back-of-the-envelope calculations from a 25 percent cycling share easily takes you to perhaps fifteen thousand lives saved every year in the UK alone.

That on its own would seem reason enough to summon the bulldozers and start building bike lanes. But there's also reduced smog and the accompanying benefits in combating climate change, many fewer families destroyed by the grief of road deaths, especially among vulnerable people like children and the elderly. You can even factor in a notable boost to overall mental health, and more vibrant local economies.

But most of all, after that magic button was pressed, you'd

suddenly find yourself among towns and cities that were suddenly more welcoming to human beings, rather than built for rapid, anonymous, one-ton metal boxes, often carrying a single person for a laughably short distance. This is absolutely not to say cars have no place in a cycle-centric imagined future, because of course they still will, even if they might end up being driverless ones. For now, however, they're used far too often and frequently for the wrong sort of trips.

In a world dominated instead by bikes, people can amble, children can play, fresh air can be breathed, conversations can be heard, all without our omniscient, noisy, smelly, lethal modern-day plague. If the woman in the visor had been driving along Lower Thames Street, chances are we could never have exchanged a smile. She would have been another impersonal head and shoulders glimpsed briefly through a windshield. Cyclists are recognizably human, traveling at human-scaled speeds. As a benefit to urban living, that can hardly be overstated.

So yes, cycling can save the world—or at the very least make it a significantly and noticeably more healthy, safe, equitable, and happy place.

And I'm not an environmental zealot, or a Luddite crank, someone who believes people should turn their backs on the modern world and embrace an antiquated technology. That's yet another paradox of the bicycle, and perhaps the most important one of all. For all that, its basic design hasn't fundamentally changed since its arrival in the late nineteenth century; the bike is almost uniquely suited to life in an increasingly urbanized modern world.

More than half the globe's population now lives in towns or cities,[3] many of which are clogged and choked by motor traffic. The bicycle can play a huge role in changing this, and in many cities is already beginning to do so. Amid the sometimes gloomy talk in upcoming chapters of public health disasters, smog-choked cities, and traffic casualties, real change is coming.

This is, above all, a story of hope.

CHAPTER 1

A Healthier World

I No Longer Trusted My Body

This book isn't a memoir. But it would never have been written without my own very personal experience of cycling, particularly the effect it had on my health. There's even a plausible argument that riding a bike saved my life. So before I describe how bikes could transform global health, allow me a brief personal detour.

It's not wholly unfair to say I was something of a runt as a child, scrawny to a degree that these days would possibly bring a family visit from a social worker. I was also affected by severe asthma, which emerged very early at age two, in the wake of a near-fatal bout of pneumonia.

As a child this never stopped me from playing sports. I was an enthusiastic if very obviously untalented footballer, but my efforts were generally sound-tracked by a slight wheeze and the voices of concerned adults asking if I should perhaps have a short break.

All this was nonetheless manageable until my late teens, when I experienced a spate of sudden and very acute bouts of breathlessness, not uncommon in asthmatics at that age. For me, these culminated in half a dozen or more trips to the emergency unit of my local hospital in suburban Cheshire, in the northwest of England. There I was swiftly injected with Aminofilin, a powerful and near-miraculous drug I only later learned can have occasional serious side effects, including heart complications. Suddenly able to breathe again, I would then spend several days begging doctors to be allowed to go home and be freed from a chest ward packed with coughing retirees smelling of tobacco.

More than once my breathlessness was sufficiently worrying for a doctor to sprint to the drugs cupboard. This is not a reassuring sight. Well more than one thousand people die from asthma every year in Britain.[1] It's far from inconceivable that I could have been among them.

As often happens with asthma, things improved gradually over time. My three years at college saw just one hospital stay. But by then I had lost confidence in my physicality. I stopped playing sports, rarely even broke into a run, and kept my spindly, ghostly pale legs wrapped in long trousers. I no longer trusted my body.

Fast-forward a few years to a large, shabby rented house in North London. Twenty-two-year-old me has pushed a chair into the middle of a bedroom and, clad in a T-shirt and a pair of extremely tight leggings, I am standing on it to examine myself full length in a large, wall-mounted mirror.

Before this vignette gets too alarming, let me explain. Three months earlier I'd suddenly given up a dull if secure graduate career to become a bicycle courier, or messenger. This was something of a surprise to friends and family, especially those who knew I'd not ridden a bike, or even done anything noticeably physical, for quite a few years.

It's hard to explain my motivation. I'm not sure even I knew at the time. An element was possibly to present myself with an inescapable daily physical challenge. "You feel let down by your body?" went the half-heard internal voice. "Now you're relying on it to pay the rent."

These days courier fashion is a staple in style magazines—the tattoos, the single rolled-up trouser cuff, the fixed-gear bike. But this was an era when the trade was generally populated by misfits, by greasy-fingered, unsocialized types who got anxious if they had to stay indoors for more than ten minutes.

Even amid this world of slight oddballs, I stood out, mainly because, knowing next to nothing about cycling, I had kitted myself with an absurdly impractical and clunky mountain bike, weighing about as much as a small moped. I rode this around London dressed in a combination of my own clothes and those borrowed from my then-girlfriend, wrapped in ever-thicker layers—I'd compounded my rashness by beginning this new, outdoor career in autumn.

The mechanics of the courier trade are fascinating. It is simultaneously a deeply exploitative industry and one where, at least in that largely pre-e-mail era, the paid-by-the-delivery earnings could be extremely high. Before long these were sufficient to pay off my student debts, a process helped by my being too exhausted to spend money on much else beyond the industrial-sized sacks of pasta on which I subsisted. More relevant is that after a few months pedaling my behemoth of a bike for about sixty miles a day, the effect was starting to show, even on a milquetoast like me.

This brings us back to the North London bedroom. A couple of days beforehand I had begun insulating my legs from the winter chill with a pair of my girlfriend's thick cotton leggings, over which I wore a pair of denim shorts (I did say the courier trade wasn't fashionable then). That evening, getting undressed ahead of the obligatory postwork bath, where I would happily steam amid a rising black tidemark of pollution residue, I decided to inspect my new look.

Then came the shock. Not from the leggings. The mirror showed those to be about as curious-looking as I'd expected. What struck me was the encased silhouette of my legs. They had always been traditionally unimpressive. A cruel teenage acquaintance once likened them to lengths of string with knots for the knees. But now they had shape. Form. Muscles. Definite muscles. I was amazed. I spent a good ten minutes on that chair, staring.

In retrospect it might sound obvious that being in your early twenties and exercising vigorously for ten hours a day makes you look and feel much better, but it was a transformative moment for my life. In the months to come I'd occasionally bump into university contemporaries as I delivered packages and, once they'd stifled their surprise that someone with a good degree from a decent university was doing such a job, many would remark on how, you know, *healthy* I looked.

I remained a bike messenger for three years, far longer than strictly necessary. This included a stint in Sydney, Australia, working for a company called Top Gun, who, perhaps believing the name alone wasn't camp enough, kitted out their riders in skintight, hot pink Lycra jerseys. If you didn't start off with some measure of body confidence, you soon picked it up. A couple of times I was on the receiving end of wolf whistles, and I still like to think they weren't ironic.

Amid this period I forgot my lifelong sense of doomed physical fragility. It was always assumed that I was the fittest person in my peer group. Friends in the pub would, after a few drinks, quietly ask to squeeze my thigh muscles. I would race buses from the traffic lights on my bike for fun. I was suddenly invincible.

Let me add some important context here: you don't need to ride three hundred miles a week, every week, or even be in your early twenties, to feel the benefits of cycling. As we'll see, even a relatively sedate daily bike commute can have a near-miraculous health impact at just about any age. And, as mentioned in the introduction, my own cycling is now closer to this more tranquil model. I'm now very much more the everyday rider. It's been some time since anyone squeezed my thigh in a pub.

Given this, I decided to see whether this more ordinary regime was still keeping me healthy. The best way to find out was to take a VO2 max test, which measures peak oxygen uptake. Expressed in milliliters of oxygen absorbed per kilo of body weight per minute, it's generally viewed as being as good a way as any to objectively measure someone's aerobic fitness, and thus their associated cardiovascular health.

And so I ended up in the sports science laboratory of the University of Kent, a large, windowless room filled with stationary exercise bikes, between which flitted white-coated technicians carrying trays of test tubes. I was there to take what's known as a ramp test, one of the more obviously sadistic procedures scientists are permitted to inflict. This saw me placed on one of the bikes and ordered to turn the pedals at a certain, constant speed while the resistance was incrementally raised, as if climbing an increasingly steep incline. The torment lasted for about twenty minutes until my lungs eventually gave out, and I reached a sweaty, juddering, breathless halt. If that wasn't enough, this was all done while wearing a clammy, full-face rubber mask, while every five minutes someone pricked my finger to extract blood and test it for levels of exertion-induced lactates.

My personal torturer/tester was James Hopker, an affable senior academic at the university, who works closely with British Cycling. The results would take a week to be processed, he told me, gently peeling the mask from my slumped form. What would happen, I thought gloomily, if the conclusion came back that I have distinctly average fitness for a man of my age? Possibly I'd give up the idea for this book.

It's Not Cycling That's Dangerous

Many cyclists will have experienced this conversation at some point. While waiting at a red traffic light, a driver, generally a man, starts chatting through the open car window. "You're brave," they will say in a convivial tone. "Wouldn't catch me cycling. Much too dangerous."

When this happens to me I usually have time for no more than a weak smile before the lights change. But in a parallel fantasy world I would discover the driver's home address and burst through their front door that evening. "Dangerous?" I would bellow, as they stumbled up from the sofa, lit by the flickering blue glow of a flat-screen television. "You think riding a bike is dangerous? It's this TV that's going to kill you." This would, of course, be vastly pompous, and risk a well-deserved punch to the nose. But I'd be right. It might sound counterintuitive, but watching television can be far more dangerous than riding around the truck-clogged streets of a major city.

One major study by researchers at the Maryland-based National Cancer Institute followed more than half a million Americans ages fifty to seventy over eight years. The key conclusion? Watching a lot of TV made people significantly more likely to die, even when you accounted for factors like smoking, age, gender, race, and education. In fact, those who watched the most TV—an admittedly Herculean average of seven hours or more per day—were 60 percent more likely to die during the course of the project than those who limited it to an hour or less.[2]

Here's Dr. Adrian Davis, a British public health expert who is a world expert on how various forms of activity affect our health: "When people say cycling is dangerous, they're wrong. Sitting down—which is what most of the population does far too much of—that's the thing that's going to kill you."[3]

That's not to claim cycling holds no risks. In many countries it's more perilous than it should be. For example, in the United States, it's about five times more dangerous than in the Netherlands, measured by deaths per billion kilometers cycled.[4] But it's also very important to not overstate the hazards. In more or less any industrialized country, the health incentives for cycling massively outweigh the perils, and provably so.

For a 2010 study, researchers from Utrecht University's self-explanatorily named Institute for Risk Assessment Sciences studied dozens of existing papers to calculate what would happen if a hypothetical group of five hundred thousand people switched overnight from cars to bikes: would the health gains from more exercise outweigh the risks from pollution and road crashes?

For the bike-friendly Netherlands the results were, as you'd expect, conclusive: on average the benefits exceeded the perils by a factor of about nine, a figure that increased as people got older. But the effect was dramatically positive more or less anywhere you looked. Even in Britain the life-extending benefits were greater by a factor of seven.[5]

When you expand this effect to a national level, any dangers from cycling, even amid the somewhat feral traffic environment of a New York City, a London, or a Sydney, become a mere speck on public health risk charts.

Every year about seven hundred Americans die on bikes, a figure that could and should be significantly lower.[6] But over the same period at least two hundred thousand of their compatriots die from conditions linked to a lack of physical activity, notably cardiovascular problems and cancer.[7] Even this is likely to be a very conservative estimate. In Britain, public health experts say, the official estimate for this inactivity toll is about eighty-five thousand a year,[8] against one hundred or so cyclists killed annually.[9] Depending on who you listen to, sedentary living is either the second or fourth most common risk factor associated with early deaths worldwide. Not far behind it is obesity, which is itself exacerbated by inactivity.

Those who chronicle these perils say that even relatively small amounts of fairly moderate exercise can slash the risks. Cycling, in particular, has been found to have an almost miraculous effect, in part because it is so easy to incorporate into everyday life, but also because it has a tendency to tempt people into slightly more strenuous effort, magnifying the advantage.

Study after study has shown that people who cycle regularly are less prone to obesity, diabetes, strokes, heart disease, and various cancers. Cyclists don't just get extra life years, they're more likely to remain mobile and independent into older age. Scientists are also only just beginning to understand the effects of exercise on our brains, and how it appears to ward off dementia.

The most comprehensive study of the health benefits of bike commuting, which we'll read more about later, found people who commuted by bike had a 40 percent lower chance of dying during the fifteen-year course of the project than those who didn't. That's not far short of a miracle. If these benefits could be administered in an injection, it would be considered one of the greatest medical breakthroughs of all time. The scientist who devised it would be a shoo-in for a Nobel Prize. Millions of lives a year would be saved. And yet it's already here.

The Pandemic of Physical Inactivity

If you ask a public health expert why cycling is so good for people, they usually begin with the inescapable contradiction that even as human lifestyles have changed beyond recognition in just the past few decades, the basic physiology of our bodies remains more or less the same as it was tens of thousands of years ago. "We are designed as hunter-gatherers, and we've not outlived our biological destiny," says Adrian Davis. "We are meant to be physically active, and within modernity we've done everything we conceivably can, it seems, to remove physical activity from our lives, down to having electric toothbrushes."[10]

The point is echoed by Francesca Racioppi, a senior policy maker at the World Health Organization (WHO), who has spent twenty years devising programs to make people more active. "We have to bear in mind that the way people live is very different to the way it was not very long ago," she says. "Once, half of us were peasants and another forty percent worked in factories, and those were physically demanding jobs. Now the vast majority of people have switched to jobs where physical activity is excluded, and we have to live with the unintended side effects."[11]

These unintended side effects are vast. In fact, it's not any sort of exaggeration to say the world faces a health catastrophe from sedentary living.

How precisely big a catastrophe depends on who you ask. The subject is complicated, not least because problems caused by lack of exercise inevitably become entwined with those connected to obesity. However, the WHO puts the annual global toll for inactivity alone at around 3.2 million people.[12] That's more or less the entire city of Berlin, dying younger than they should, every year. About nine thousand people a day. On a very gloomy WHO league table of what kills most people around the world, inactivity is fourth, beaten only by high blood pressure, tobacco, and excess blood glucose. But some experts think even this is an underestimate.

Ahead of the London 2012 Olympics, revered medical journal *The Lancet* ran a special issue devoted to what it termed the "pandemic of physical inactivity." One of the papers, led by I-Min Lee, a Harvard professor of epidemiology—the study of population-wide health trends—went further than the WHO estimates. It calculated that inactivity causes between 6 and 10 percent of cases of heart disease, type 2 diabetes, and breast and colon cancers, killing around 5.3 million people a year, about the same number as tobacco.[13]

That's not the population of Berlin, it's the population of Norway.

To get the grips with the science behind all this, I asked Dr. Justin Varney, head of adult well-being for Public Health England, what would happen if I were to hypothetically give away my bike and spend most of the next few years sitting on a sofa watching television. My mitochondria, the "engine houses of your individual cells," as he calls them, would get increasingly sluggish. Before long the cells would not function so well, making me more prone to some cancers, notably bowel cancer.

Then there are the telomeres. These tiny strands of protein in our cells gradually shorten as part of the aging process, but this process seems to be slowed by staying active (and also, Varney added, by meditation—that's believed to be one reason why you see so many ancient Buddhist monks). Scientists still don't quite understand how it happens, but the simple answer is that if I stopped exercising I'd age more quickly. Finally, by being active, I get my blood pumping faster, properly oxygenating my organs. Varney eloquently describes it thus: "If you imagine your blood like a flowing stream, the faster it moves the more it moves out all the crud in your system."[14] The combined effect of my inactivity marathon would eventually place me at far greater risk of everything from high blood pressure to heart disease and cancer.

My hypothetical experiment has, in a way, been replicated on a vast level in the world's most populous nation. During China's recent and rapid economic development, millions of its citizens stopped cycling and walking and suddenly began to drive. As late as the mid-1980s, cars were virtually never seen outside a few cities. Now there are more than 150 million of them. And the effect is being felt. Researchers on one city, Shanghai, tracked the lives of seventy-five thousand women from 1997 to 2004, finding that those who still cycled for transport had 35 percent less chance of dying over the study period than even their previously healthy peers who were less active.[15]

Even limited exercise can bring significant results. Francesca Racioppi describes a recent WHO project carried out with Oxford University to quantify the overall health benefits of even just the minimum of physical activity. It concluded that just reaching the very modest WHO recommended level—more on that in a second—cuts your overall chance of dying early by 10 percent.

"This isn't a huge amount of exercise," she says. "It's just moderate things like walking or cycling, meeting the basic WHO guidelines. But 10 percent is massive, a very important effect. If this was a pill, people would say it was a miracle."[16]

Cars Make You Fatter

This idea of activity as a wonder drug is one you hear a lot. And yet this miracle pill is, relatively speaking, quick, easy, and pain-free to administer. The official WHO threshold of being physically active for adults is doing 150 minutes of moderate exercise a week, or half an hour a day, five days a week. By "moderate," they really do mean moderate—it includes things like brisk walking, gardening, or housework. The official WHO table lists around a dozen examples, also including "traditional hunting and gathering" and "thatching a house."

The WHO's more technical definition of "moderate" is three to six metabolic equivalents, or METs, which means expending between three and six times as much effort as you would by just sitting down. This isn't a huge amount. Jogging can easily reach ten or twelve METs of effort. By happy coincidence, a slow trundle on a bike tends to equate to about five or six METs.

Even if you're not a roof-thatching hunter and gatherer, 150 minutes a week doesn't sound like a huge amount. And yet vast numbers of people simply don't do it. Professor David Buchner spent nine years in charge of physical activity for the Centers for Disease Control and Prevention, chairing the group that wrote the US government's official guidelines on the subject.

"It's a major public health issue in the United States, as it is globally," he says. "If you want to have round, ballpark figures, about 50 percent of adults in this country do not meet the guidelines."[17]

The US guidelines match those of the WHO—at least 150 minutes a week of moderate exercise, or twice that for even more benefit. But, as Buchner says, almost anything does some good. "The truth is that if everybody in the country added ten minutes a day, it would have a huge public health effect," he says. "It's a very steep dose-response curve at the low range of physical activity. We don't want the public to misunderstand that if they don't get up to high levels they won't get the benefit. They just need to start doing a little bit more, and they'll start getting more benefit."

But a lot of people aren't heeding this advice. The WHO says about a third of all adults worldwide are insufficiently active.[18] Some of the statistics are almost shocking. The national travel survey carried out by Britain's Department for Transport has found that people make a third fewer trips on foot than they did in 1995. A fifth of all people say they haven't walked more than twenty minutes even once in the past year.[19]

Additionally, as health statisticians wearily note, even in the era of activity trackers on phones and other fitness gadgets, most data is still self-reported, meaning the scale of the problem is almost certainly even greater than this. It is in part why some experts are setting their targets very low. Justin Varney and his team at Public Health England are currently trying to persuade people to do just thirty minutes of moderate exercise a week. That might seem remarkably little—just walking half a mile three times a week would do it—but even this modest effort can bring impressive results.

"If we get everyone to one hundred fifty minutes, fantastic," he said. "However, I come from a pragmatic school of thought. If we can get the entire population doing at least thirty minutes a week, which is not scary for people, that would have a significant impact on the burden of ill health in this country."[20]

Others set more ambitious goals. Professor Wendy Brown from Queensland University led the team that compiled Australia's current physical activity guidelines. These advise people to aim for twice the WHO recommendation—three hundred minutes of exercise a week, or an hour a day five times. Brown explains this as a response to the parallel public health scourge of obesity in Australia, a country now ranked as the fourth fattest in the developed world. "One of the things about us is that there's a perception we're a nation of active, bronzed Aussies—surfing, being on beaches, and things like that," Brown says. "In reality we're actually much more a nation of sports watchers."

The three-hundred-minute goal was an attempt to "push the range." She explains: "We advise that if you want to avoid weight gain it has to be an hour a day. We're the only ones in the world so far, but I reckon it won't be long before others follow."[21]

The WHO calculates that more than a third of all adults worldwide are overweight or obese. In a first for human history, significantly more people are now dying from eating too much than too little. The health consequences are almost beyond comprehension. In Britain, the National Health Service (NHS) spends about £16 billion a year treating conditions associated with obesity, especially type 2 diabetes, the form of the disorder often associated with excess weight and inactivity.[22] In 2014, the head of England's health service said obesity could soon bankrupt the NHS, calling it "a slow-motion car crash in terms of avoidable illness and rising healthcare costs."[23]

Obesity is a slightly more tricky area for this book, since it's arguably caused as much by diet, especially the modern ubiquity of cheap, high-sugar, high-starch convenience foods, as well as other factors. But physical activity does play a key role in maintaining a healthy weight. And there's another, less-known connection: overweight people who exercise tend to be far more healthy than their slim, inactive peers.

Justin Varney explains: "There's more and more evidence that if you're fat and fit you're healthier than someone who is a healthy weight and sedentary. Your best option is to be a healthy weight and to be physically active. But if you're an unhealthy weight, being active will significantly reduce the risk of things like diabetes and coronary heart disease, and reduces your mortality."[24]

There is increasing evidence that being inactive is, in fact, more deadly than being overweight. One huge recent study, led by Cambridge University, traced more than three hundred thousand European men and women over twelve years, seeing what impact both of these had on their health. It extrapolated the findings to estimate that of 9.2 million deaths in Europe in a given year, about 337,000 could be attributed to obesity. The number blamed on physical inactivity? A total of 676,000.[25]

At the same time, cycling is a great way to ensure people don't become overweight in the first place. One landmark study saw academics follow the health of five thousand people in eight provinces around China from 1989 to 1997, a period when many households bought their first-ever car. Even after adjusting for diet and other factors, men who acquired a motor vehicle for the first time gained on average nearly four pounds of weight more than those who didn't.[26]

It seems that cars make you fatter.

The Benefits of Accidental Exercise

Now that we've outlined this huge, worldwide problem, the obvious question occurs: why is cycling the solution? In part it's down to a phenomenon known as "incidental activity." Guaranteed to make a public health expert prick up their ears, this is based around the idea that people are far more likely to be physical if the exercise is integrated into their everyday lives rather than being an artificial extra.

"When we say, 'Go to a gym,' that's discretionary time," explains Anne Lusk, a public health expert at Harvard University who specializes in ways to get people cycling. "You have to eke that time out of your week, which includes not being with your spouse, not being with your children, tending to your house or job. Yes, it's good to go to the gym. But, boy, is that hard time to carve out of your already packed day."[27]

This is where the bike comes in. Riding a bike as a means of transport has the wonderful capability to create physical activity while also, given sufficiently safe and connected cycle lanes, being fun and saving you time. This is the key, the experts say. Ashley Cooper, professor of physical activity and public health at the University of Bristol in the UK, a man who has spent more than twenty years warning governments about the perils of sedentary living, describes active travel as "probably one of the best bets for improving population-level physical activity."

Cooper describes being summoned a couple of years ago to see the UK's chief medical officer, the government's most senior health adviser: "He asked what the answer was to physical inactivity. I told him it's about creating an environment in which active travel is easily doable. It has to become a habit rather than a chore. There are numerous trials where people are told to go out and walk, and they're not sustainable. People don't go out and do it if there's no purpose to it. But if it's everyday transport there's evidence that when people stop for a period, for example because of winter, or an illness, they're likely to return to it."[28]

By "active travel," Cooper and others do of course mean walking as well as cycling. Regular walking can also greatly assist your health, even if the benefits, as we'll see below, might be less dramatic. But cycling has another big advantage—you can travel farther. Even riding pretty slowly, most people can cycle a three-mile commute in about twenty minutes. On foot it could take an hour. That means a lot of workplaces are easily reachable by bike.

The UK government has particularly detailed data on work travel patterns drawn from the once-a-decade national census. The latest figures, from 2011, found that even as average commutes are gradually increasing, half of all working people still travel less than three miles to work. More than two-thirds of people live less than six miles from their work.[29]

Of course, many people commute longer distances, especially outside Europe. Also, not everyone will want to cycle three or six miles each way to their job, even if they are in a country with safe and connected bike lanes. But the potential is still huge, especially with the rapid growth in the use of electrically assisted bikes, or e-bikes. Even if just one in ten car commuters got on two wheels, that's a lot of people getting their daily dose of activity. The picture is similar in many other countries. And with more than half the globe's population now living in urban areas, the overall scope is unimaginably vast.

There is another key reason why cycling is such a good fit for the inactivity crisis: an increasing bulk of evidence shows that riding a bike brings notably greater health benefits than even the WHO-approved regime of walking, gardening, and roof thatching. Push yourself that little bit harder, and a little longer, and the dividends multiply. Riding a bike, especially to and from a job, or a school or college, generally involves the exertion of setting off from traffic lights, or riding up a hill, and can often last more than half an hour a day.

Scientists are not prone to hyperbole, but Dr. Adrian Davis calls the benefits of bike commuting "amazing." He says: "It's really because of the vigorous element you often get in cycling, which you don't get in other activities—it raises the heart rate over a certain threshold, strengthening the heart's function. If you're going at a moderate pace, you're doing your moderate physical activity, which is fine, but it's the vigorous which will provide you with much greater protection by time."[30]

One common problem with walking is that it needs to be fairly brisk to count even as moderate exercise, a point many people miss. Anne Lusk points to studies showing US dog owners actually tend to weigh more than the national average. "People have been saying for a long time, 'Gee, I'm going for a walk to the dog park, that's good,'" she says. "Your dog is exercising in the dog park. You're not. You're walking slowly, or standing and talking to friends. You're at one MET." In contrast, she explains, it's much harder to not exert yourself on a bike. "I always joke that you can't bike slowly, as if you did you'd fall over," she says. "When we have a bad day we can all walk slowly."[31]

Along with lower weight, cycling brings astonishing improvements to cardiovascular health. One of the more straightforward if gloomy studies involved a doctor at Northern General Hospital in the north of England examining the autopsy reports of thirty-two regular cyclists who had died in various ways and comparing their hearts with those of noncyclists of the same gender and similar age. Those who'd ridden bikes, he found, had a very significantly lower incidence of blocked arteries or other coronary obstructions.[32]

The most famous and exhaustive research of its kind is the one mentioned at the start of the chapter. Perhaps inevitably it took place in Copenhagen.

Led by Lars Bo Andersen, an epidemiologist at the University of Southern Denmark, it charted the lives of more than thirty thousand Danes of all ages over an average of fifteen years, during which almost six thousand of them died. Even factoring in things like noncommuting exercise levels, it found those who biked to work were 40 percent less likely to die during the study. Forty percent. If you tried to skew the odds so much your way in a casino, they'd throw you out for cheating.[33]

The Barnet Graph of Doom

Callous as it might sound, while the idea of physically inactive people dying young is a worry to government ministers, it's the thought of the inactive ones who stay alive for decades that really keeps them awake at night. This is the notion of morbidity, simply meaning the quality of health experienced by people, especially as they age. It's a question ultimately of money, especially the costs connected to people who become debilitated by illnesses from sedentary lifestyles but, in part due to medical advances, are still able to live long lives.

Most industrialized countries are facing a looming health-related catastrophe when it comes to public finances. Their populations are aging, with all the medical complications this incurs. At the same time, more and more people are acquiring expensive-to-treat conditions like type 2 diabetes at an ever-younger age. Britain's Royal College of Physicians summed it up bluntly: "Current costs of providing healthcare cover for a physically inactive ageing population are not sustainable."[34]

It's not just about direct medical costs. There is also the problem of paying for more and more care for people increasingly unable to look after themselves as they age. The crisis this has brought is summarized in something known, in all seriousness, as the Barnet Graph of Doom. While in fact the most prosaic of things—a dull-looking chart taken from a local government PowerPoint presentation—a glance at it is enough to prompt an involuntary shudder in most senior government officials.

Drawn up a few years ago for a speech by the chief executive of Barnet, a council on the northern edge of London, it portrays two elements: rising bars showing the projected cost of the authority's future statutory social care obligations into the coming years, and a gently declining line for the predicted budget over the same period. At some point in around 2022, the two meet. If this were to happen, there would be no money left for anything else. No libraries. No swimming pools. No parks. Not even refuse collection.

The Graph of Doom can be dismissed as one of those oversimplified models that happen when you extrapolate current trends without factoring in possible changes. But it's still a fantastic exemplar of the scale of official worries about poor health later in life. About two-thirds of the forecast costs on Barnet's graph come from adult care, much of which is taken up with older people unable to look after themselves.

The key point is this: the less active someone is when they're younger, the more likely it is they will eventually need expensive assistance, such as visiting nurses or a place in a residential home.

This is a connection Justin Varney regularly makes to prod people into taking up exercise: "I tell them, 'Being active throughout your life is about being able to get to the loo on time in your old age.' It does resonate. They can get their heads around that. It's about dignity as much as anything else."

Given all this, are countries where a lot of people cycle invariably healthier? The short answer seems to be a qualified yes. A 2008 study in the *Journal of Physical Activity and Health* compared rates of active travel in two dozen nations—comparing the prevalence of cycling, walking, and public transport to obesity levels. The headline results were striking. The nations with the most active transport—the Netherlands, Switzerland, and Latvia—had the lowest obesity rates. Meanwhile the United States had the least amount of active travel (12 percent) and the most obesity (34.3 percent at the time selected).[35] It is, inevitably, more nuanced than this. The study used figures collected variously between 1994 and 2006, and some of the data was self-reported and thus potentially of mixed quality. Also, physical activity is just one part of the public health picture. Denmark, for example, has higher than average smoking and alcohol consumption rates.

That said, more cycling can bring a series of almost accidental benefits for countries. Research in Denmark has found that when people start riding a bike, they also often then begin eating a better diet and cutting back on alcohol and tobacco. "Taking up the bicycle as a mode of transportation for work seems to have an effect on your wider lifestyle," says Bente Klarlund Pedersen, one of Denmark's best-known public health experts.[36]

From another major cycling nation, the Netherlands, comes a more curious example still. "In grocery shops here we don't have a lot of the gallon packages for soft drinks and juice," says Saskia Kluit, head of the Fietsersbond, the Dutch cyclists' association. "The reason is that a lot of people cycle and they can't be transported as well on a bicycle. It's not anybody consciously thinking, 'We should only sell one-liter packages.' It's just a positive interaction."[37]

The next frontier of physical activity science appears to be the brain. The ability of exercise to alleviate depression, stress, and anxiety is already much documented. Less well known is its apparent boost to overall cognitive function.

"In some sense this is not even understood by science yet," says David Buchner. "The most recent consensus reports have a lot of interesting evidence on the effect of physical activity on the brain. They haven't quite sorted it out yet, but I would expect over the next ten years it will be. It'll have implications both for diseases of the brain, like Alzheimer's, and academic performance in children."[38]

You Should Be Reading This Book Standing Up

As a warning for any fit and healthy cyclist currently reading this book from the comfort of an armchair or sofa and feeling even slightly smug—there is another area in which science is making new strides over sedentary living. Studies show that even regular, vigorous exercise doesn't completely insulate you from the perils of sitting down for long periods.

This is, Ashley Cooper explains, partly due to the fact humans have particularly big muscles in their legs. If you fail to use these for an hour or so at a time, then the cells can undergo a process known as "downregulation," meaning they produce less of certain proteins. This, in turn, is associated with poorer cardiovascular health and worse handling of glucose, increasing the risk of diabetes.

"There's quite good evidence in adults that, regardless of activity level—unless you're a completely mad athlete—then high and prolonged levels of being sedentary is associated with worse health outcomes," Cooper says. In simple terms, he explains, it means that even if you're a regular cyclist and you sit down at home to watch a couple of hours of TV in the evening, he'd recommend you get up every twenty minutes or so, to make a cup of tea or just stretch your legs.[39]

While this remains a relatively new development, it's notable and sobering that almost every time I've phoned a public health expert for this book they were talking from a standing desk.

Theresa Marteau, a Cambridge University professor who studies the interaction between public health and the environment, not only has a standing desk in her office, she has another one for meetings. Research into their benefits remains at an early stage, she says: "What we're particularly interested in is what happens during a twenty-four-hour period. If there's any kind of compensatory behavior, for example people then go home and lie down a lot, that's not so great. But I like to think that in twenty years' time we will find it unbelievable that people spent hours sitting down."[40]

And if by some chance you ever make a speech to a room of public health experts and, when it ends, they all stand up to clap, bear in mind it might not necessarily be that you're such an amazing orator. They could be thinking of their health.

"It's called active applause," says Ashley Cooper. "Very popular in the physical activity world. They tend to be complete believers. If you were to go to one of our conferences you'd find about half the audiences would be listening to the presentations standing up. It's a very hot topic."

So should we be worried that the people who know the most about the perils of inactivity are themselves a bit nervy if they sit down for more than about half an hour?

Yes, we probably should.

It barely needs to be pointed out that combating physical inactivity involves more than just people buying a bike. For the world to reverse this pandemic it will require a host of changes to people's lives, and to the way homes and communities are designed around them. Such open social engineering tends to prove controversial, but it's been done before. In the 1970s, Finland had the world's highest rate of heart disease, partly due to inactivity, but also smoking and poor diet. Now, after decades of huge, community-based programs to promote change, rates are 75 percent lower.[41]

It's hard to overstate the potential impact if governments undertook similarly ambitious attempts to create mass cycling. Cars are among the main factors associated with inactivity. Even if the globe's tech companies, as expected, usher in an imminent new era of efficient electric vehicles that drive themselves and never crash, you're still left with the problem of a sedentary, ailing population.

So why aren't government ministers across the world crowbarring open the doors to municipal sheds so they can commandeer bulldozers and start carving bike lanes into every available mile of road space? Why are cities not already populated by fleets of healthy, two-wheeled citizens, cheerily pedaling their way to, and past, their 150 minutes per week?

This is, for the most part, a question connected to political inertia, powerful vested interests, a lack of real ambition and leadership from governments, and a set of curious but persistent and damaging myths about cycling and cyclists. These are issues to be addressed later in the book, but it's worth noting that public health experts believe change is coming, even if it might still take time.

"The amount of attention and funding that's paid to tobacco control is much larger in the United States than is paid to physical inactivity," notes David Buchner. "One of the issues with physical activity is it has to have this coordinated response across sectors. It's not public health that builds the roads or the parks, or puts physical education in the schools. It takes this larger consensus to get things to happen in multiple areas of our lives."[42]

Francesca Racioppi agrees. "It's a relatively long path we

need to take," she says. "So many interests need to be convinced that investing in cycling is good for them. Consider that we've known about tobacco as a risk factor for fifty years. It took about forty years until governments started to introduce things like smoking bans in public places. It all takes time."[43]

According to Justin Varney, the moment might finally have arrived: "In western countries there is a kind of sense that the time has come for physical activity as a preventative factor we can do something about. It's fun, it's free or pretty cheap, it's easy, anyone can do it. It's starting to happen."[44]

And what of my personal experiment? The Kent University lab results arrived in my e-mail a week later, as promised, in the form of a very professional-looking three-page report. It even had a chart. Luckily for this book, the headline finding was that my VO2 max is fifty-three. This isn't anywhere near professional level—some top cyclists can reach the high seventies—but it is, Hopker explains, "considerably above" the normal range. The average for a man in my early middle age is nearer thirty-five.

Delighted, I spent several days browsing specialist exercise websites featuring VO2 max comparison tables. Some of these, pleasingly, suggested my aerobic capacity is that of a fit man in his early twenties. My favorite table is that which places me in a category labeled "superior."

It's possibly overdramatizing the narrative to say cycling saved my life. But it's no exaggeration at all to say cycling transformed it. Much as the sudden seriousness of my teenage asthma was simply terrifying, the arguably bigger obstacle was the retrospective sense that I was physically incapable, substandard, helpless. Being active changed this, permanently, and in a remarkably short time.

CHAPTER 2

A Safer World

The Death of Simone Langenhoff

On the morning of October 14, 1971, Simone Langenhoff set off from her family's rural house near Helvoirt, a village in the southern Netherlands, to cycle to her school. The trip, just over a mile down a narrow, tree-lined road, was one she made every day, usually with one of her five older sisters—but on this occasion she was alone.

As Simone pedaled along that autumn morning, a woman drove her car at high speed around a blind bend and plowed into the girl, killing her. Simone Langenhoff was six and a half years old.

Almost forty-five years later, Simone's elder sister Anita says she recalls little of the precise circumstances of the crash. But she is very clear about the effect it had on her family.

"There is a story that the woman had been drinking the night before, but I'm not certain," Anita says. "Afterwards, my father was very angry, though he never talked to us about it. My mother went to a hospital, from grief. She had a breakdown. And our father just thought about his work. The family fell apart." Soon, Anita explains, her parents divorced. The five surviving sisters remained with a mother who never properly recovered from the loss: "We children were on our own. Not only because of the accident. But the accident changed everything."[1]

Such pointless deaths, and the spiraling agony which follows in their wake, are still depressingly routine. Around the world, about 1.25 million people a year are killed on roads, almost 3,500 every day. A quarter of these are pedestrians or cyclists.[2]

But in one respect, Simone Langenhoff's death was special. Her father, Vic Langenhoff, was a prominent journalist with *de Tijd*, or the *Time*—a Dutch daily newspaper. Heartbroken at the loss of his youngest child and enraged at the 150-guilder fine imposed on the speeding driver—slightly under $50 at the exchange rates of the time—Langenhoff set about highlighting the human consequences of a booming postwar car culture in the Netherlands, traditionally a nation of cyclists. Over the previous twenty years, as the total miles driven per year in the country had increased fivefold, road deaths also rocketed, from about 1,000 in 1950 to 3,300 in 1971. Among the 1971 fatalities were 450 children, one of them Simone Langenhoff.

Every day, her father discovered, twenty-five more Dutch children were injured by vehicles—almost half of them while riding bikes. His country was, Langenhoff calculated, the most dangerous place in the world for child traffic casualties.

He began to meet other concerned parents around the Netherlands. Then one of his older daughters, age ten, was hospitalized along with four friends after a speeding driver forced them off their bikes. It was time for action.

On September 20, 1972, Langenhoff used a full page in *de Tijd* to announce a new road safety pressure group. The name was revealed in a dramatic banner headline: "Stop de Kindermoord," or "Stop the Child Murders." The organization was, he wrote, "trying to break through the apathy with which the Dutch people accept the daily carnage of children in traffic."

Langenhoff unleashed his months of grief and fury on "the criminals" in regional governments, who were busy redesigning the roads for the new fleets of motor vehicles without thought for those who, like Simone, had no choice but to walk or cycle.

"This country chooses one kilometer of motorway over one hundred kilometers of safe cycle paths," he wrote. "There's no pressure group? Let's start one. Parents of little victims, worried parents of potential little victims: unite."[3]

That's precisely what they did. Langenhoff's article galvanized the fears and anger of millions of Dutch people who resented the sudden and unannounced tyranny of these anonymous, deadly metal boxes. Stop de Kindermoord turned swiftly into a major protest organization. Its members used innovative, direct-action tactics like staging mass "die-ins" and occupying busy roads, turning them into impromptu play streets.

As Langenhoff stepped back from the front line, others took over. The group's first appointed president was Maartje van Putten, a young student and mother who lived near one of Amsterdam's new, busy arterial roads and watched in alarm from her apartment window every morning as young schoolchildren tried to cross it.

She and the group set about agitating for better cyclist and pedestrian provision. "We used to block streets at rush hour," says van Putten, later a member of the European parliament. "We stood hand in hand in a circle. That, of course, would get us on the radio and in the papers. Soon enough we'd get the pedestrian crossing light we wanted, or the cycle lane. It became normal that people were doing those things across the country."[4]

The politicians gradually started to listen. There was an unexpected boost with the 1973 oil crisis, which saw gas prices suddenly quadruple, prompting governments to question the anticipated future in which the car was the dominant form of transportation. More support came two years later with the formation of the very vehemently named First Only Real Dutch Cyclists' Union.

Gradually, miles and miles of bike infrastructure was built and the cyclists started to come back. Now almost 30 percent of all trips in the Netherlands are made by bike, many more in urban areas. In Amsterdam, almost half of all city center journeys are on two wheels. In Utrecht this figure is 60 percent.[5] The eventual Dutch method of separated bike lanes and tamed vehicle traffic has proved the model around the world.

It's possible none of this would have happened without Stop de Kindermoord. Most other European nations stuck with the supremacy of cars for several more decades, leaving bikes as the niche domain of hobbyists and die-hard devotees. In contrast, the Netherlands gradually, painstakingly reengineered its streets to allow everyday people to ride ordinary bikes for routine tasks, without notable danger or intimidation.

Cars were not banished. The Dutch own slightly more per head of population than the British, though still some way behind American or Australian levels. But these are less likely to be used for short, single-person urban journeys. About nineteen thousand miles of separated lanes insulate cyclists from fast-moving motor vehicles.[6]

The Dutch now see slightly under six hundred traffic deaths a year, fewer than a third of whom are cyclists.[7] Barely any children are killed, generally fewer than half a dozen.

As for the rural road on which Simone Langenhoff died, in many ways it still looks the same as her father described in his newspaper article: narrow, laid with paving slabs, and lined by tall oak trees. But now it has smooth, separated lanes behind the trees on both sides, allowing people to cycle or walk in safety. The modern-day Simones can ride in perfect peace of mind.

It's fair to argue the changes begun by Vic Langenhoff saved many thousands of lives. He died in 1997, and spoke little in his later years about Stop de Kindermoord. But Anita Langenhoff, now fifty-six, finds it hard to even consider the positive repercussions from her sister's death, an event she says she still thinks about every day.

"It had such an effect on the whole family," she says. "Can I think about anything positive coming from it? No, no. Personally, no. For other people maybe. But not for us."[8]

Fear, Near Misses, and Why Road Culture Matters

Writing about the tyranny of road danger is a potentially tricky area for a book devoted to mass cycling. It's important to reiterate that even in many nations without anything approaching Dutch or Danish levels of cycle infrastructure, riding a bike is considerably safer than many people commonly believe. Even in Britain, where a mere 1 or 2 percent of all trips are made on a bicycle, the average person would ride two million miles before they faced even a serious injury.[9] So why scare people?

The simple response is that they're already scared. Study after study has shown that the number one reason most people don't cycle is because of a fear of motor traffic.

One of the most famous investigations of this phenomenon was a 2010 report from a research team who spent months in four British cities, interviewing dozens of families in depth about their travel choices. Almost all said the same thing: they could not imagine riding a bike in such overwhelmingly car-oriented urban layouts.

Even more experienced riders often saw the roads as "a dangerous obstacle course," wrote Dr. Dave Horton, who led the three-year study: "The minority of people who cycle in

English cities tend to do so despite, not because of, existing conditions," he noted. "Some people try cycling, but are quickly put off."[10]

A later UK research project delved more deeply into this environment of intimidation. The 2015 investigation, led by Dr. Rachel Aldred—a transport academic who specializes in cycling—found that while actual injuries might remain fairly rare, fear and alarm are near-daily companions for far too many riders. Her self-explanatory Near Miss Project saw around 1,500 UK cyclists fill out website diaries about their on-the-road cycling experiences on a single day chosen by them in advance.

The findings were shocking. While the frightening incidents recorded varied in seriousness, from a driver overtaking too closely to someone deliberately driving at them, more than 80 percent of people said they experienced at least one on their given diary day. The study calculated that "very scary" events were a weekly ordeal on average, with almost three-quarters connected to motor vehicles.[11]

"I was in the cycle lane," began one entry from a female rider in Bradford, in the north of England. "Lorry comes up behind and starts hooting, not once but repeatedly, and revving his engine. I swerved, he got past, I caught him up at the next red light so it was entirely pointless. Terrified."[12]

You could ask almost any cyclist in places like the UK, the Unites States, or Australia and they'd have dozens of similar tales. A few days before writing these words I was cycling to my office when a construction truck overtook me far too close on a main road, the driver honking the horn as he went past to mark his displeasure at my not cycling in the gutter. All of fifty yards later he was obliged to stop for a red light.

I caught up and spoke to him as calmly as the adrenaline allowed: that was intimidating and scary. If the shock from the horn blast had made me wobble, I could have fallen off onto the pavement, or worse, under the wheels of the truck. I'm a human being. Why? He stuck out his tongue and rolled up the driver window.

There now exists the beginnings of a pushback against this frightening road culture, notably through the Vision Zero movement. Begun by Sweden's government in the late 1990s with the lofty intent of working toward a road environment in which no one dies, it has now been embraced to varying extents in other countries, often with cyclists at the forefront. In the United States it gained particular prominence when New York City mayor Bill de Blasio adopted it in 2014 with a ten-year target for eliminating traffic deaths. However, critics note that this deadline currently looks set to arrive about thirty years later than that.

What is behind this culture? The simple answer is normalization. Even in the relatively cosseted modern world of richer countries, where fatal epidemics are rare and bad, and workplace injuries a cause for lengthy investigation, killing or maiming someone on the roads is still seen as tragic but inescapable. It is, to use a ubiquitous and linguistically poisonous term, an "accident."

This in turn fuels a complacent, entitled, careless driving

culture, where millions of people who would see themselves as moral, kind, and careful people nonetheless get into a motor vehicle and routinely, unthinkingly, put others' lives in peril.

Like the truck driver who skimmed me, the great majority of these incidents don't actually hurt anyone, but often this is down to pure chance: a driver's assumption that a cyclist won't swerve because of a bump in the road, or will brake in time for a car turning across their front wheel. Worst of all, such maneuvers are pointless, particularly in cities, where cyclists almost always catch up at the next junction. When it happens to me I try to ask the driver why they did it. The response can be outright hostility. More often than not it's just bafflement.

This complacency comes from a mind-set in which some deaths are seen as more notable, more avoidable, than others. The normalization of road deaths is so embedded it can be shocking to survey the contrast. Between 2001 and 2013, 3,380 American citizens died due to terrorism at home or abroad, the great majority in the September 11 attacks.[13] Over that same period a shade over 501,000 people died on US roads, or the cumulative terrorism total roughly every month.[14] One much-quoted study suggested that the decision of many US travelers to switch from air travel to driving in the wake of September 11 brought about around 1,500 additional road deaths.[15]

Those killed in road crashes don't have a permanent memorial or a museum, or a Department of Homeland Security with a $38 billion annual budget aimed at making sure it never happens again. At most, some are commemorated by loved ones with a cross or other marker at the place where they died.

This is the extra poignancy behind the story of Simone Langenhoff. Remarkably few other traffic deaths prompt such public outrage or national self-examination. In the overwhelming majority of cases, while families are torn apart by grief, society at large continues as if nothing much has really happened.

The Thousand-to-One Chance

In the early 1950s, when the death toll on Britain's roads was almost three times higher than it is today despite vehicle numbers being just 15 percent of the modern total, Alan Lennox-Boyd, the minister for transport in Winston Churchill's then-government, said something very wise about auto crashes.

"Accidents in the main arise from the taking of very small risks a very large number of times," he said. "A thousand-to-one chance against an accident may not be rated very high, but for every thousand people that take it there will be an accident."[16] Little did Lennox-Boyd know how personally prescient were his words. Three decades later, at age seventy-eight, he was trying to cross Fulham Road, a busy thoroughfare in West London, when he was hit by a car and killed.

The slightly unpalatable fact is that more or less everyone

you know who drives a motor vehicle will routinely take such thousand-to-one risks, half-conscious acts that, even if they don't kill a retired politician or a six-year-old child, help keep our cities and streets off-limits for many people. If you drive, you probably do it, too.

This might sound as if I'm a militant antidriver. I'm not. Over the years I've owned various cars, as well as a couple of captivating if unreliable camper vans. That said, I'm generally happier not owning a car, in part because of the inevitable, unrelenting expense, but also because every time I sit behind the wheel I'm agonizingly aware that this is the one time in my everyday existence where there's a real, if statistically slight, chance that I could take a life.

This just doesn't happen when you get on a bike. It could, but barring a turn of events considerably rarer than winning a lottery jackpot, it doesn't. Significantly more British people die on average each year due to stings from bees or wasps than from a bike hitting them. Quite often the figure is zero.[17]

People don't change their personality when they get off a bike and into a car. It's simply that the risks you take in a vehicle can have appallingly magnified consequences. It's not morals, it's just physics.

Consider that most prosaic of things: distraction. I'm not immune to this on a bike. In my early teens, in an incident that went straight into family legend, I cycled down my hilly home street while fiddling with a loose cable that ran between the bike's front wheel and a clunky mechanical speedometer. Inevitably I rode straight into the back of a parked postal van. I was briefly stunned and spent a night at the hospital for observation. My bike was bent beyond repair. But the van was barely damaged and the postman himself, who was sitting in the front sorting letters, suffered nothing more serious than the shock of hearing a loud bang and finding, on investigation, a slightly confused schoolboy tangled up in a twisted bike frame.

I'm by no means alone. One of the curiosities of riding a bike around a Dutch city is the apparent inability of local teenagers to cycle without simultaneously checking their phones, even sending text messages one-handed. But this generally happens at little more than 10 mph, and on a dedicated bike lane. Serious repercussions happen, but they are rare.

In contrast, according to US government figures, 3,154 people died on American roads in 2013 due to crashes connected to distracted drivers. Of those killed, around 450 were pedestrians or cyclists.[18] The US National Highway Traffic Safety Administration makes the chilling calculation that at any one moment of daylight across America about 660,000 drivers are looking at a phone or another electronic device.[19] Teenagers are, inevitably, the most likely age group to kill themselves or others in a car by not paying attention.

Another of Lennox-Boyd's routine thousand-to-one risks is high speed, as Vic Langenhoff knew, to his endless sorrow. Leah Shahum, a former cycling advocate who now heads the Vision Zero Network in the United States, says limiting vehicle speeds is "the biggest factor" in reducing deaths. "That's not something we've talked a lot about in America," she says. "If we at Vision Zero Network were only to achieve one thing—I hope we do more—it would be to help communities effectively manage speed."[20]

That speeding is dangerous is both much debated and, when you look at the evidence, utterly irrefutable. One particularly tenacious academic, Rune Elvik, from Norway's Institute of Transport Economics, has spent much of his career perfecting a statistical analysis known as the Power Model. This takes actual data from more than a dozen countries to estimate by how much road casualties increase given a certain rise in traffic speeds.

When a few years ago Britain's government mooted raising the speed limit on the country's motorways from 70 mph to 80 mph, Elvik was able to inform them that, even assuming a conservative 3 mph rise in actual speeds, they could expect about twenty-five more deaths and one hundred serious injuries a year.[21] The plan was soon dropped.

And yet speeding remains ubiquitous. About two-thirds of American drivers admit to regularly exceeding speed limits,[22] with similar statistics in the UK. This isn't just an issue for freeways or rural main roads. A series of streets around me in southeast London have been designated 20 mph zones by the local council, mainly a theoretical aspiration given the lack of enforcement. One of them has a digital signboard telling drivers how fast they are actually going. I've spent ten minutes at a time there and not seen a single vehicle adhere to the limit.

In part, this is because most speeding is semi-officially tolerated. License plate–recognizing speed cameras remain illegal in many US states. In Britain the top-selling newspaper, the *Sun*, ran a recent campaign seeking to force police using radar speed guns to wear high-visibility jackets to give drivers proper warning of their presence.[23] They have not, as yet, suggested that police offer the same courtesy before they search people for knives, which kill considerably fewer British people each year.

Why do so many people tolerate, even encourage, putting others in danger? Again, it comes down to culture. Those seeking more equality on the roads are battling almost a century of motorist-led propaganda arguing that the deaths of cyclists and pedestrians is not just unavoidable but, in many cases, somehow the fault of the victims.

Murder Most Foul and Blaming the Victim

In 1935, the year British drivers first had to take a test to be allowed on the roads, the secretary of the Royal Society for the Prevention of Accidents (RoSPA), set up twenty years earlier amid rapidly increasing traffic deaths, addressed a meeting of the organization.

"Animals have now developed a road sense, but children must still be trained," argued Colonel A. A. Pickard. "Thirty years ago dogs preferred to take their nap in the middle of the road. Hens invariably flew across the road in front of your car. The chicken of today, however, hatches out with an instinct of road sense. It flies into the hedge, not into the road. Dogs are equally wary. You will see them look before crossing. They recognize the warning of the horn and stop, or even get back to the pavement. But it may be many generations before babies are born with a road sense instinct."[24]

In that year, 6,502 people were killed on Britain's roads. Of these, just 196 were drivers. Another 1,400 were cyclists, and just over 3,000 were pedestrians. About 75 percent of pedestrian fatalities involved either children or people over sixty.[25] This was a one-way massacre, and yet even RoSPA, an organization officially dedicated to road safety, seemed to believe it was up to the victims to adapt for the convenience of their killers.

Pickard's speech is quoted in one of the most righteously furious publications about death on the roads. *Murder Most Foul*, written in 1947 by the largely forgotten J. S. Dean of the Pedestrians' Association pressure group, spends an eloquent if occasionally melodramatic 114 pages denouncing "the motor slaughter" and, in particular, the pervasive message that it was somehow not the fault or responsibility of drivers.

"The more the drivers kill and maim the more right they become, and the more right they become the more dangerously they drive," Dean wrote. "Or, to put the position from the opposite side, the more the non-drivers, and especially the pedestrians, are killed and maimed, the more this is proof of their carelessness and refusal to be 'educated,' and the more this is accepted the less care is taken by the drivers to avoid them, and this is applied to the youngest children and the oldest and most infirm persons."

Dean was scathing about the efforts of supposed road safety groups like RoSPA, particularly the message that rather than placing the obligation on drivers it was up to children to learn road sense from infancy. "Put the idea of death and destruction deep into their minds," he wrote. "Never let them forget it. Fill their lives with it. Teach them fear. Make them frightened and keep them frightened."[26]

All this would be a historical curiosity were it not for the fact that many of these attitudes remain, albeit expressed less bluntly. The modern road safety message in many countries, especially to children and young people, is still based around encouraging them to wear bright colors, emphasizing that they must endeavor to be seen, rather than the responsibility falling on drivers to travel at sufficiently slow speeds and look out for people.

Worse still, the evidence seems to be that rather than such advice making cycling and walking any safer, it just seems to make it less common.

One highly influential early examination of this phenomenon came in 1990, when Mayer Hillman, a maverick architect-turned-campaigner for livable cities, examined what he saw as a fundamental contradiction in the official narrative about traffic safety in the UK. On one hand, proudly quoted official statistics showed the rate of child traffic deaths per vehicle on the road had decreased by 98 percent since the 1920s.[27] At the same time, Hillman noted, the government was running a fear-based traffic safety campaign aimed at young people, showing someone about to step off a curb with the slogan "One false move and you're dead." Which was correct?

To untangle this paradox, Hillman and his colleagues at the Policy Studies Institute think tank replicated a series of surveys carried out by the same organization in 1971 into how much children were allowed to walk and cycle unsupervised. With increasing economic prosperity, cycle ownership had actually risen among younger schoolchildren over the period, they found, from two-thirds to 90 percent. But while in 1971 almost 70 percent of children with bikes were allowed to ride them on the roads, by 1990 this had plummeted to 25 percent.[28] Far fewer children walked unaccompanied, especially to school.

This was not an era of greater safety for children, Hillman concluded; it was one of greater confinement to the home. "The 'good old days' of reminiscence and the 'good new days' depicted by the accident statistics are reconciled by the loss of children's freedom," Hillman concluded. "The streets have not become safer, they have become, as the government's poster proclaims, extremely dangerous. It is the response to this danger, by both children and their parents, that has contained the road accident death rate."[29]

A US-led study into the subject from 2009 found a similar picture in America. While in 1969 almost 90 percent of US children who lived within a mile of school would walk or cycle, by 1999 this had dropped to 30 percent. The researchers found a much-celebrated 70 percent decrease in child pedestrian fatalities was matched by a 67 percent decrease in walking to school.[30]

Society had been rebalanced to favor the motorist, wrote the authors of this study, titled "Who Owns the Roads?" "Soon after the automobile's creation, its proponents worked to reconstruct the meaning of safety, removing the connection between speed and danger," they said. Even language had adapted, they noted, with words like "jaywalker" coined to describe those who "failed to show deference to the motorist by walking where and how they always had."

This tilting of the odds away from vulnerable road users is so institutionalized that many people don't even realize it's there. A small number of people, however, find themselves obliged to face up to this culture of indifference, usually for the most awful of reasons.

How to Get Away with Murder

In June of 2000, police arrived unexpectedly at Cynthia Barlow's office in London. Her daughter, Alex McVitty, had been crushed by a cement truck that overtook and turned across the twenty-six-year-old as she cycled to her job at a law firm. The appalling grief of so suddenly and violently losing her only child was not even the end of Barlow's ordeal. She soon found that she was facing a police and justice system that appeared to care little for such deaths.

The truck driver, who said he had not seen Alex in his various mirrors, was charged with dangerous driving. Before the trial Barlow asked repeatedly to be warned of any distressing evidence, and was assured there would be none. She then arrived at the court on the first day to find a TV screen set up to play graphic security camera footage of her daughter's last moments.

The prosecution's evidence seemed strong, but when questioned in court over a key element of the incident, a policeman admitted he couldn't read his own writing in his notebook. The driver was acquitted.

"I got to the end of all the legal processes in a state of absolute despair," Barlow says. "My experiences had changed me completely. Nothing was going to be the same, ever again. The trust you instinctively have in the system was all gone."

Barlow decided to fight back. She bought shares in CEMEX, the construction materials firm whose truck killed Alex, so she could attend its annual meeting and ask directors how they would make their vehicles less likely to kill cyclists in the future. CEMEX is now at the forefront of such safety efforts, including driver training and extra mirrors, sensors, and alarms in truck cabs.

As with the aftermath of the tragedy that hit the Langenhoff family in 1971, it's very likely that Cynthia Barlow's actions have saved other lives. But like Anita Langenhoff, when asked if this might be a reason for some pride, Barlow seems barely able to understand the question. "I'm not interested in me," she says finally. "What matters is my daughter."[31]

To make another comparison with the story of Simone Langenhoff, part of the horror of Barlow's experience is how unexceptional it is. Because traffic deaths are seen as everyday and inescapable, law enforcement and judicial systems often treat them as accidents even when they are very clearly not. This inbuilt set of assumptions seems all the stronger when the victim is a cyclist.

Shortly before this chapter was written, two cyclists died

in quick succession in crashes in Brooklyn. Lauren Davis, thirty-four, was struck by a Fiat car in the morning rush hour on a narrow one-way street. Later that day New York police officers briefed reporters that Davis had been "salmoning"— riding against the traffic flow—and hence the Fiat driver was not investigated. Five days later, James Gregg was crushed by an eighteen-wheeler truck. The first police account claimed the thirty-three-year-old had been holding on to the vehicle to propel himself along and fell under a wheel. Local media duly carried reports about both incidents as being tragic but largely self-inflicted.

There was one problem: none of this seemed to be true. A witness emerged who had been riding behind Davis before the crash, moving with the traffic, not against it. She said she saw the Fiat turn across Davis into a side road.[32] With Gregg, the police soon dropped the claim about him holding on to the truck, and then speculated that "wind force" had sucked the young man under the wheel.[33] Neither police statement about Gregg's death mentioned that the truck driver, legally, should not even have been driving on the residential street.

This phenomenon of automatically ascribing fault to vulnerable road users was investigated in a hugely depressing academic study from New Zealand, which focused on the death of an unnamed ten-year-old girl who was struck by a van and killed while trying to cross a road on her way back from school one Wednesday afternoon.

The first police report concluded the girl had run across the road "without any warning." There was, it added, no suggestion of excess speed by the driver, who was said to be traveling at about 40 kph.

However, a civil engineer sent to examine traffic on the road at the same time a week later found speeds were, on average, 8 kph above the 50 kph limit. The volume of traffic allowed pedestrians just a four-second gap to cross. Running was the only option.

Despite this, the subsequent, brief inquest fully endorsed the police view. The coroner speculated the child might have "been doing a little bit of jaywalking." Such a phrase, noted the Auckland university researchers, "clearly signals negligence on the part of the child."

They added: "Structural contributors, in particular the causal factors pertaining to the transport system, emerge from this process of moral arbitration unscathed. Poverty, the volume of traffic, the lack of provision of safe places to cross, and, particularly in this case, the state's inability to enforce its own speed limits, are ignored."[34]

There is a well-known adage among the worldlier breed of British police officers: *If you want to get away with murder, do it in a car.* Looking at cases like the death of Alex McVitty and the New Zealand schoolgirl, it is hard to disagree. Had the CEMEX truck driver been so inattentive on a construction site, he would most likely have faced manslaughter charges under workplace safety laws. If the girl, who would now be in her thirties, had been killed by more or less anything else—a knife, unsafe food, a faulty gas heater—the investigation would have been much more thorough.

This bias continues into the court system, particularly when juries become involved. Under the English legal system, if you're accused of certain traffic offenses—for example, causing death by careless driving—you are allowed to decide whether the case is heard by a magistrate sitting alone or at a higher court, with a jury. A magistrate can jail you for six months at most. If you're convicted by a jury, the sentence can be five years.

And yet, most canny lawyers advise their clients to opt for a jury trial. Why? Because juries are notoriously wary of convicting drivers. Martin Porter, a leading personal injury barrister who is also a keen cyclist, says driving offenses "seem far more likely than other serious crimes to invoke empathy and compassion from a jury."

" 'There but for the grace of God go I' is not a thought likely to cross many jurors' minds with murder, rape, terrorism, or knife crime," he says. "But surveys show that a majority of drivers admit to breaking speed limits, and almost all can probably remember a lapse in concentration or worse when in a car."[35]

Even if a driver admits guilt or is convicted, the penalties are often laughably low. A 2014 analysis of data from forty-five UK police forces found that of all the drivers convicted in connection with incidents in which a cyclist was killed, just 44 percent received any sort of jail time. More than a quarter were not even banned from driving.[36]

It is, in fact, surprisingly difficult for drivers to lose their licenses in many places. Under the UK system drivers receive "points" for infractions, ranging from three for minor offenses to ten or more for, say, driving while drunk. If a driver amasses twelve points, they should normally have their license suspended for a period.

However, magistrates have the discretion to not do this if, for example, they believe a person badly needs to drive for personal or work reasons. An investigation in 2013 found people still allowed on the roads despite amassing more than thirty or forty points. One man had been caught speeding eight times in little more than two months, but he was still driving legally, the researchers found.[37]

It's not hard to see the repercussions of this. One study of California court statistics by epidemiologists at UCLA found that drivers with prior citations were almost four times more likely to hit a child pedestrian than a randomly selected control group. This rose to more than thirteen times more likely for those with five or more citations. It might seem obvious that such people are more likely to cause harm. What's arguably most shocking is that the majority of them were on the roads by right: 83 percent still had a valid license.[38]

With the legal odds stacked so strongly against them, it's little surprise so many people choose not to ride a bike.

Banishing the "Accident"

In recent years some people have begun to challenge this lexical approach. In 1993, Leonard Evans wrote an editorial in the *British Medical Journal* (*BMJ*) explaining why "crash" was a better word than "accident." Eight years later he won the argument, and the *BMJ* banned the use of "accident" for road crashes. "An accident is often understood to be unpredictable—a chance occurrence or an 'act of God'—and therefore unavoidable," the *BMJ*'s North American editor Ronald M. Davis wrote. "However, most injuries and their precipitating events are predictable and preventable."[39]

The approach of Vision Zero is similar: to see road deaths as something that can be analyzed, predicted, and thus eventually eliminated. "When you map out where the severe and fatal crashes are, you often see trends," says Leah Shahum. "It's an unfortunate trend, but it's often very helpful. City after city you have these concentrations of dangerous areas. For instance, in San Francisco, seventy percent of the severe crashes happen on twelve percent of the streets."

While dozens of other cities have become interested in Vision Zero, Shahum says, none have as yet become as involved as San Francisco and New York. "It's early days," she says. "It will take time. It needs leaders to say that we're going to need to do things in a dramatically different fashion. It doesn't just mean doing a little bit better, working a little bit harder."

What's often not sufficiently appreciated is that creating streets that are more welcoming for cyclists has a wider safety dividend for other road users, particularly pedestrians. More bikes and fewer cars will create, to use the title of this chapter, a safer world.

Again, this is nothing to do with a supposed greater skill or moral rectitude of cyclists. It's just physics, or more precisely kinetic energy—the force generated by motion. Kinetic energy increases exponentially as the object involved gets heavier and more rapid. As an example, consider me riding my solid, everyday bike at 12 mph. If some hypothetical inattention meant I hit a pedestrian, they would face kinetic energy of about 1,250 joules. That's not insignificant, but it could be much worse. Had I been driving the last car I owned, a relatively tiny Nissan MICRA, the energy imparted of that traveling at 30 mph would have equated to just short of 100,000 joules. Make it a midsized SUV at 35 mph, and suddenly we're at almost 270,000 joules. It's a very different impact.

Of course, predicting what happens in a particular real-world collision is impossible. Pedestrians, and other cyclists, do die when struck by a bike, usually as a result of a secondary impact—for example, their head striking a curb as they fall. It happens, and is no less unimaginably tragic than any other road death. But it is also rare enough to be a much-reported news story when it does take place.

The other transformational safety effect concerns motor traffic itself. As we'll see in chapter 5, a general prerequisite for mass cycling is not just separated lanes for bikes on faster routes but low vehicle speeds on quieter streets, typically no more than 20 mph and often less. It can be difficult to embed, but when this lower-speed system works there's suddenly a lot less kinetic energy around to kill or injure people.

The precise effect of reduced driving speeds on pedestrian deaths is much debated, but there's no doubt it is significant. One examination of casualty data from the UK and Germany found the risk of fatal injury to a pedestrian was between 3.5 and 4.5 times higher for a car traveling at 40 mph rather than 30 mph.[40] A US road safety group found the death rate for pedestrians is 2.3 percent for cars traveling between 10 mph and 20 mph. At 40 mph or more, 54 percent of people are killed.[41]

As you might expect from all this, countries like the Netherlands and Denmark generally have good road safety records by global standards, although there are other factors at work—for example, tough drunk-driving laws. One apparent curiosity is Britain, which despite a near-nonexistent cycling culture has an identical road fatality figure to the Netherlands, with 2.8 fatalities a year per one hundred thousand people.[42] How is this so? In part, it appears, this is because the benefits of safer traffic have not been shared equally.

British statistics for the number of people killed or badly injured on the roads show these almost halved over fifteen years, from forty-two thousand in 1999 to twenty-four thousand in 2014. But closer examination shows by far the biggest reduction came among drivers or passengers, and to a lesser extent among pedestrians. For cyclists, the absolute number of deaths and injuries was almost the same in 2014 as in 1999, without overall cycling levels having notably increased.[43]

A decade and a half of massively improved road safety mainly benefited people inside vehicles, not those who needed the help most.

I Woke to Find Myself in a Dark Wood

This unequal battle on the roads has become gradually acknowledged in recent years. An official world day of remembrance for traffic victims every November was begun in 1993, and is now officially recognized by the United Nations.

The idea came from RoadPeace, a British charity set in 1992 by Brigitte Chaudhry, whose twenty-six-year-old son had been killed by a driver running a red light. Its pioneering campaigns focus particularly on the most vulnerable people, the victims of what RoadPeace calls "traffic homicide." Amy Aeron-Thomas, the group's executive director, argues that even campaigns like Vision Zero neglect this element of injustice.

"We do think there should be more priority given to reducing the threat of death, injury or even intimidation to others than to yourself," she says. "If you look at the collisions between cyclists and cars or pedestrians and cars then you see that the pain and suffering is all on one side."[44]

More than a decade and a half after her daughter's death, Cynthia Barlow is the chair of trustees for RoadPeace, and a respected national figure on traffic safety. But things could have been very different.

In the wake of the farcical court case that saw the acquittal of the driver who killed her child, Barlow says, she was seriously considering suicide. A concerned friend took her to see an exhibition of Botticelli's drawings for Dante's *Divine Comedy*.

"At the entrance to the exhibition was a big picture of the first words of the poem: 'Midway along the journey of our life I woke to find myself in a dark wood,'" Barlow remembers. "I kept going back to the exhibition and let my brain do what it was doing. Eventually I realized I was suicidal because I blamed myself for what had happened to my daughter's case. I realized it wasn't my fault, it was the system. Out of that came an absolute, unshakeable determination that things were going to change."[45]

Changing this system will be slow. Every day, around the world, there are new Simone Langenhoffs, new Alex McVittys. But the change will come. It must.

CHAPTER 3

A More Equal World

It's a slightly unusual sight. In the shadows of a block of flats in Overvecht, one of the poorer suburbs of Utrecht, a dozen or so women wearing head scarves are cycling slowly around the perimeter of a parking lot. For one section of the loop they try to remain within a pair of lines chalked on the asphalt, causing a couple to wobble alarmingly.

This is a cycling lesson with a difference. The students are middle-aged women from Moroccan and Turkish back-grounds, communities that began arriving in the Netherlands from the 1960s but have, in one slight respect, not completely integrated into national life.

That area is cycling. Utrecht likes to consider itself the cycling capital of the world's most bike-mad nation, with 60 percent of trips in the center made on bikes.[1] But some of these women have lived there for decades without being tempted onto two wheels.

Naima, forty-seven, who stops for a chat after negotiating the chalk lines, drawn by a tutor to mimic the width of one of Utrecht's ubiquitous bike lanes, says she came to the Netherlands from Morocco twenty-seven years before, but never learned to ride a bike, in part because the Moroccan community remains more car-focused than average.

But having started the lessons, Naima says she feels transformed. "Being able to ride a bike means I can go cycling with my children—they cycle everywhere," she says. "I can do the shopping on it, and go and see friends. But also, being able to ride a bike makes me feel more Dutch, more part of the community."

Dennis Schoonhoven, who organizes the class, along with about a dozen other similar ones, on behalf of the Harten voor Sport community organization, says the aim is more than simply helping the women feel they belong. "It's not just about integration, it's about emancipation," he argues. "In these communities, sometimes the role of the women can be very much based around the home, and they're afraid to travel too far. But when they know they can ride a bike they are suddenly free."[2]

Arguing in favor of better cycling facilities from the point of view of equality or social justice can be a difficult one. If you already ride a bike in Britain and some similar countries, chances are you already sometimes face people assuming you're somehow being smug, even superior. "Oh, very green," they'll half joke as you arrive, helmet in hand. "Look at me, just an ordinary, fallible person with my car." It's a strange attitude, not least as in my experience most people ride a bike because it's convenient and fun, rather than to make a point or save the world. As such, you rarely hear people making pro-bike arguments explicitly based on societal or environmental reasons. And yet, the more you examine these ideas, the more compelling they seem. As bold a claim as it might sound, cycling can make societies notably fairer.

It comes down to the fact that the bike is arguably the most equal and democratic form of transport in existence, at least in an urban setting. It is nearly as cheap as walking, and in some ways is arguably more inclusive, not least because—as Naima discovered—a bike can greatly expand your physical and social boundaries.

Cycling has an amazing ability to heal social divides, to act as a particularly effective community glue for people who are otherwise the travel-deprived, and thus often the most cut off. If there are safe, coherent bike lanes, children are far less reliant on a parent being a chauffeur. Older people who struggle to walk a long distance or are wary of driving can possibly still use a bike, especially a modern, electrically assisted machine. Women are far more likely to cycle. Many people with disabilities can use handcycles or other adapted machines that they might not wish to ride amid heavy traffic.

And then there's the issue of cost. Transport can take a significant chunk of households' budgets. In the UK it's an average of about 15 percent.[3] In America this rises to 19 percent, and then 25 percent in areas where people are most dependent on cars.[4] This can create considerable hardship for many people. If cycling is suddenly possible for local journeys, this burden eases greatly. And yet, in another curiosity of the subject, poorer people can sometimes find themselves excluded from cycling.

Such effects are magnified all the more when you consider the current reality. The deeply unjust truth is that in thousands of cities, from London to New York to Shanghai to Delhi, transport is mainly built around cars, and thus explicitly for the benefit of the richer-than-average minority who disproportionately own them. More than this, the external social costs of driving tend to fall predominantly on the less prosperous, who are more likely to live near a main road, enduring noise and smog, with their community bisected by busy traffic.

This happens almost everywhere, and most people don't even notice it. In my area of inner southeast London, census figures show about 60 percent of households don't own a motor vehicle.[5] And yet the streets are dominated by vehicles, whether parked or driving past, pumping out fumes, creating noise and danger, to the detriment of everyone.

Enrique Peñalosa, the mayor of Colombia's sprawling, chaotic capital city of Bogotá, built hundreds of miles of protected bike lanes, arguing that they are vital to equality. "They are a right, just as sidewalks are," he said. "They are a powerful symbol of democracy. They show that a citizen on a thirty-dollar bicycle is equally important to one in a thirty-thousand-dollar car."[6]

A Dawn of Emancipation

One of the more curious-seeming social justice divides in cycling is gender. There's no obvious reason why a woman can't get around on a bike just as easily and happily as a man. But it's there. Of the cyclists I see on my regular commute in London, I'd guess about a quarter are female. That would be near the UK average, where 29 percent of bike rides nationally are made by women and girls.[7] In the United States it's 24 percent,[8] and 21 percent in Australia.[9] Focus in more locally and the anomalies can get more jarring still. Britain's 2011 national census found that of 397 self-professed bike commuters in Burnley, a town of nearly one hundred thousand people in the northwest of England, just 6 percent were female. That's twenty-four women.[10]

You get a hint as to the likely reasons for all this when you look at the gender split for cycling in some other countries. In Germany it's more or less even. In Denmark and the Netherlands, a small majority of cyclists are female, at 55 percent and 56 percent, respectively.[11] Having a more equal gender split for cycling, it seems, depends on possessing some decent cycling infrastructure. This relationship appears time and again, even within the same city. A survey in New York found that on one street with a protected bike lane, 20 percent of cyclists were female. On an adjoining street with no lane, the proportion fell to 10 percent.[12]

There are several theories as to why this happens. One factor seems to be that women are more likely to make complex, multistop trips than men. Travel surveys show they disproportionately carry out other duties beyond commuting— for example, also dropping children at a school or nursery, or grocery shopping. If you've got a simple one-person, one-stop ride to work, then cycling swiftly amid the traffic before having a shower at the office might seem a good idea. If your journey involves a child seat or even a cargo bike, it's suddenly much less appealing.

There is also a hypothesis that women face more risk riding in heavy traffic in cities. This is based on the slightly contentious idea that women tend to ride less assertively than their male peers, keeping more to the edge of the road, meaning motor vehicles, notably trucks, are more likely to try and squeeze past or turn across them. One London news-paper calculated that from 2009 to 2015, thirty-three women were among the eighty-four adult cyclists to be killed in the city. This amounted to 39 percent of the fatalities, despite the fact that women make up 25 percent of the London riding population. But more glaringly, of the women killed, twenty-seven of them were hit by trucks, more than 80 percent of the total, against less than half of the men who died.[13]

Another element of this could be that female cyclists, on average, tend to ride more slowly than their male counter-parts, prompting more impatience among drivers when they are obliged to share the same space. My entirely unscientific household evidence suggests there's something to it. My girl-friend, a self-professed dawdler on the bike, comes home several times weekly complaining of a driver turning across her front wheel or otherwise cutting her off. It does happen to me, but noticeably less often.

The Near Miss Project, mentioned in the previous chapter, brought up some evidence that women face disproportionately more of this intimidating driving when on the road, experiencing roughly twice as many frightening incidents per mile as men. The academic behind the study, Dr. Rachel Aldred, believes this could possibly be connected to slower cycling speeds. "That did come up in the comments, when people reflected and said, 'You have to go really fast,'" Aldred explains. "And that is my experience, too. If you're cycling more slowly, more sociably, you potentially do face greater hostility than if you're able to keep up with motor traffic, and not be overtaken quite so much."

This is unpleasant stuff, and all the more troubling given the noble, if now sometimes forgotten, role of the bicycle during the early days of female emancipation.

In her intriguingly titled 1895 publication, *Lady Cyclist*, the English writer Louise Jeye was effusive about the craze enjoyed by increasing numbers of mainly middle-class women. "This is a new dawn, a dawn of emancipation, and it is brought about by the cycle," she wrote. "Free to wheel, free to spin out in the glorious country, unhampered by chaperon or even more dispiriting male admirer, the young girl of today can feel the real independence of herself, and while she is building up her better constitution she is developing her better mind."

This was part of a wider social revolution that followed the invention of the first modern-looking bike, the "safety bicycle," in the late 1880s. With its ease of mounting and

pneumatic tires, it was far more practical than the penny far-
thing, and the safety bicycle became hugely popular in a
number of countries—especially for countryside rides along
routes as yet unbothered by motor traffic.

The British biologist Professor Steve Jones once described
the bicycle as the greatest-ever invention to combat genetic
disorders, since it gave people who previously tended to only
marry those within walking distance of their homes a new
opportunity to woo and mate with a far greater variety of
potential partners.[14]

For women, cycling helped loosen the constraining social
mores of the Victorian era as well as, more literally, loosen
their restrictive Victorian outfits. People as varied as the early
US suffragist and rights campaigner Elizabeth Cady Stanton
and, in Britain, the countess of Malmesbury, used the advent
of the bike to argue for what was known as "rational dress"—
a change from the regime of corsets and whalebone-hooped
skirts.

In *The Eternally Wounded Woman*, a book about women
and exercise in the nineteenth century, Canadian academic
Patricia Anne Vertinsky describes how doctors initially
praised the cycling craze as an answer to sedentary female
lives. Inevitably, before long the profession then began to
worry about overexertion, and the effect of saddles on re-
productive organs. There was even a diagnosis of something
called "bicycle-face" among bike-mad women: staring eyes,
a strained look, and "a general focusing of all the features
toward the center." Overall, however, concludes Vertinsky,
the bicycle "did more perhaps than any other activity to

form new conceptions of what it was possible for women to do."[15]

And so, in 120 years of cycling, we have moved from Louise Jeye's emancipated Victorian ladies spinning out freely in the countryside, to their twenty-first-century successors wondering if they can cycle fast enough to avoid being intimidated. It's not exactly progress.

How Everyone Can Cycle

Troels Andersen, the head of cycling projects for Odense, where about half of trips in the city center are made by bike, is describing one of the social benefits from decades of investment in cycle facilities in the Danish city. "It's very rare that older people stop cycling because of the infrastructure and safety, it's mainly because of balance problems," he notes. "With some people, when they can't cycle anymore because of their age, they push their bike along as a walking frame, leaning on it. They don't like to use a normal walking frame, as then you look really old and frail. They walk around the city with their bike, and they feel normal."[16]

The idea of older people still so wedded to using a bike is almost entirely absent in countries without safe cycling routes. A 2008 study found the average elderly Dane is thirty times more likely to cycle than his or her American counterpart. And while the statistics for older cycling in Denmark are fantastic, in the Netherlands they become truly astonishing. Levels of cycling only began to drop after the age of seventy, and even at the age of eighty about 20 percent of all trips are made on a bike.

As well as the usual health improvements, cycling in older age appears to bring extra benefits. One Australian study from 2013 found older people who cycled regularly had significantly improved leg strength and balance, reducing the likelihood of a debilitating fall.[17]

There is also a very big social gain. As with the women learning to cycle in Utrecht, a bike helps older people stay connected with others, which is less likely to happen if cars are the only option. A US study found that about a fifth of Americans above age sixty-five don't drive. Such people make 65 percent fewer trips to see friends and family than those with use of a car.[18] In contrast, older Dutch people arguably have more options than ever, thanks to the increasing popularity and affordability of electric-assist bikes, or e-bikes, which give a helpful nudge from a small electric motor when the rider pedals. More than 20 percent of the near-million bikes sold each year in the Netherlands are now e-bikes.[19]

Saskia Kluit, director of the Fietserbond, the Dutch cyclists' union (hers is the successor organization to the First Only Real Dutch Cyclists' Union of chapter 2) says e-bikes have helped keep older people cycling, and expand the area they can reach. "And it all becomes a lot more fun," she says. "You can get to friends who are further away, to the forest and seaside. Because they can go further they will go further. And it's a big social motivator, keeping them connected to children, grandchildren, friends—whatever."

Many Dutch people cut back or halt driving in their mid-seventies because they don't feel confident behind the wheel, Kluit explains: "But then they will increase their cycling. That's the difference from other countries. Even in Denmark, people tend to stop cycling aged sixty or maybe seventy. We cycle far into the seventies, even the eighties."[20]

Similar patterns appear at the other end of the demographic scale. In Odense, more than 81 percent of children ride to school.[21] The city's aim is for bike routes to be sufficiently safe for all children ages six and over to ride alone. I repeat— to ride alone, age *six*.

In the United States, by contrast, the most recent annual study by the National Center for Safe Routes to School found that even for students living between one and two miles away, a distance rideable in little more than fifteen minutes, just 2 percent of them cycle. Around half are driven.[22] In the UK, between 2 percent and 3 percent of students ride.[23]

Travel to school is just one element of childhood freedom. Dr. Alison Carver, a public health and transport expert at Deakin University in Melbourne, has led various studies into the limited ways children in Australia and the UK are allowed to get around. One 2013 paper found children who walked or cycled independently to school had significantly more "mobility license" to get about during other parts of their lives.[24] She has also found that children who live within three miles of a dedicated bike lane are twice as likely to cycle to school as those who do not.[25]

This can have implications beyond independence and the

ability to see friends. Carver has found that cycling is a particularly good way to boost exercise levels in teenage girls who might be wary of competitive sports.[26] But without safe spaces to cycle they often miss out.

This subject strays into all sorts of complex areas connected to the wider debate about cosseted, screen-bound, inactive children and the greater freedom granted to earlier generations. But there's little doubt that safe cycling makes life more connected when you're young.

I have very personal experience of this. I spent three years as a child living in Copenhagen, after the company my father worked for sent him for a stint in their Danish office. We had no connection to the country, and no family tradition of cycling, beyond the usual British childhood experience of riding bikes around parks or on sidewalks.

But as soon as we moved to Copenhagen, when I was nine, my sister, brother, and I all cycled to school. In fact, we cycled everywhere. I'd ride to see friends, to and from soccer practice, to the local shops. There were bike lanes in many places, and where there were not, drivers knew to expect cyclists on the roads. It never occurred to me, or my parents, that I wouldn't be safe.

And then we moved back to the same English town we'd left three years earlier. It was far smaller, but without bike lanes and with streets again dominated by fast-moving cars. The cycling more or less stopped. Once again I was reduced to getting lifts from my parents. Until my sudden, future decision to become a cycle messenger, cycling played an increasingly small part in my life.

If cycling as a mobility aid for children and older people is neglected in many places, when it comes to people with disabilities the general assumption is often that this is an actual conflict. In London, disability is regularly used as an objection to new bike lanes. "How's someone in a wheelchair going to travel about?" they ask. "What's the use of a bike lane for them?"

These people have never met Isabelle Clement. Until her midthirties she would hardly ever go into central London from her home in the south of the city because of the difficulties of parking her car, which she saw as the only viable way to get around. But when her young son started riding a bike, Clement, seeking to keep pace with him, bought a clip-on attachment for her wheelchair that turns it into a handcycle, a three-wheeled device where you pedal using your arms. Now she can park just outside the city center and ride the rest of the way, an even easier task since she upgraded the handcycle addition to one with an electric-assist motor.

Clement, who lost much of the function of her legs following a spinal tumor in infancy, is impatient with the assumption that people with disabilities do not want to cycle. "I'm not naturally sporty," she says. "If I can do it, anybody can. If we can banish the assumption that disabled people can't cycle because it's just too complicated, that will help nondisabled people reengineer their own possibilities. Impairments matter less than attitude."

Clement is director of Wheels for Wellbeing, which helps

disabled people to ride. There has, she says, not yet been anyone who has come to the charity whom it has not been able to assist. However, Clement adds, many people are put off by having to share space with motor traffic, especially as handcycles and similar machines generally move more slowly than traditional bikes: "There are many perfectly good reasons why a lot of disabled people don't cycle, but they're not about the physical possibility of cycling. They're about all the usual barriers around cycling, plus some additional complications."[27]

In contrast, handcycles are seen fairly often in Dutch cities, where the bike infrastructure is designed to also accommodate them, avoiding narrow barriers or stepped curbs. Seville in southern Spain, which built seventy-five miles of separated bike lanes in one go a few years ago and saw cycling levels increase elevenfold (more on this in chapter 5), has wheelchair symbols painted on them to show their dual use. "We suddenly made a lot of the city easily accessible," Manuel Calvo, who designed the network, said with some notable pride.[28]

Getting Their Voices Heard

Layered on top of all these various inequalities is another, more generalized one: income disparity. This can, again, seem a bit anomalous when it comes to cycling. Beyond walking, riding a bike is the cheapest form of travel there is. Surely money is no barrier?

Again, there are a lot of factors at play. Some are fairly straightforward. For example, poorer people are more likely to live in apartments than houses, making bike storage potentially difficult. Some London councils have tried to address this by replacing the occasional street car parking space with a key-accessible covered shelter for about a dozen bikes.

Also, many cities have seen their inner neighborhoods gentrified in recent years amid an influx of younger, professional people attracted to the idea of living in walking or cycling distance of their workplace. These are the districts most likely to see new bike lanes, but by the time this happens many less wealthy people will have been priced out. This phenomenon has even seen the arrival of new bike lanes tied to concerns about gentrification, especially cities like New York, San Francisco, and London, where rising housing costs have socially transformed many neighborhoods.

Yet another element is that without good bike infrastructure, cycling tends to be an activity for the enthusiast rather than the everyday rider, and these are often middle-class people riding relatively expensive bikes. A research paper for Transport for London (TfL) in 2011 noted that the city's cyclists at the time were typically white, male, under forty, and with medium-to-high household incomes.[29] The statistics were used by many opponents of London's first separated bike lanes, saying that to build them was an unequal use of resources.

But there is a compelling rejoinder to all this: the moment you build cycling facilities across a city, these distinctions tend to disappear. The hobbyists are subsumed by a wave of people riding simply because it's convenient. In places like Denmark and the Netherlands the bike lanes are filled with people of both genders, all ages, most ethnic backgrounds and every social class, from members of the royal family downward.

The same pattern seemingly holds true elsewhere. A more recent Transport for London study in early 2016, following the advent of some better bike routes, found black and minority ethnic Londoners were now just as likely to be regular cyclists as white people in the city.[30] Paul Steely White, a longtime bike advocate who heads the Transportation Alternatives campaign group in New York, says new bike lanes there have also broadened the range of riders. "If you look out of your window and see who's bicycling, increasingly it looks like a good cross section of New York City," he says. "Ten years ago it probably wasn't so much the case. You'd see a lot of white hipsters and yuppies. Now it's much more of a variety."[31]

One historic criticism of bike advocacy in places like America and the UK is that it has tended to be dominated by the more vocal, privileged riders, and can neglect what are known as "invisible cyclists." These tend to be people from very low-income households who ride to their jobs because they have little other option, yet rarely appear on official statistics, let alone arrive outside city officials' offices lobbying for safer bike routes in their communities. In the United States, census data shows the group most likely to cycle (and walk) to work are people with household incomes below $10,000 a year—that is, the very poor.[32]

In the last few years, both bike advocacy groups and their backers in city governments have become more aware of this issue, particularly in America. Minneapolis, a city with well-documented income and racial divisions, is about to embark on a plan to build almost 150 miles of protected bike lanes. Lisa Bender, who cofounded the Minneapolis Bicycle Coalition before jumping the fence to become an elected city council member, says these are designed to run to poorer, more distant neighborhoods, as well as the better-off inner suburbs.

Bender explains that earlier in her career, she worked for a nonprofit organization that carried out transport projects in developing nations. As part of this, she was taken on a tour of a newly rebuilt former slum area of Bogotá by none other than Enrique Peñalosa. He proudly pointed out that there was a smooth, paved route for bikes and pedestrians, but just a dirt road for cars, Bender says: "Enrique made the point: 'We made this choice intentionally. Cars don't need paving, and this is a poor area—most people don't drive anyway. So we prioritized putting the money into the bicycle and pedestrian lanes.'"

Bender adds: "It was a moment that really stuck with me. How you spend money as a city or a government really shows your values, shows what you are investing in. That's really influenced how I do my job now."[33]

One of the cycling advocates thinking most deeply about the link between human-friendly streets and affordable transport is Tamika Butler, head of the Los Angeles County

Bicycle Coalition since 2015. "There's a lot of folks here in LA who, for a number of different reasons, just can't afford cars, or aren't able to drive," she says. "There have been a lot of people biking, walking, and taking transit in LA that sometimes were invisible. What is happening now is there is a little bit of a culture shift and those folks are starting to get a little bit more attention, and their voices heard."

Butler concedes that until recently her organization was seen as mainly serving the needs of "the white guy who has the money to buy the nice bike and the nice kit." She has a background in social justice and legal advocacy, and says she perhaps sees the world differently. "I travel through the world as a queer woman of color, in a very racist society, and so the things that are floating to the top of my list perhaps may be a little different. I don't think that makes me a worse bike advocate, I think it makes me a better bike advocate. It allows me to have different perspectives."

This job of the cycle campaigner, Butler argues, is not to "come in on your bike as a white knight saying, 'We're here to save the day.'" Talk of bike lanes, she says, must be part of a wider narrative about other inequalities connected to things like employment and relations with the police.

"It's definitely a long game, and it's going to get uncomfortable," she says. "I'm sure there're some long-term members who are asking, 'Why are we talking about social justice?' Some of them have talked to me, and it's possible it's not going to be for everybody. But if you know what's right, and you know it's important to hold the course, you sign up for a long process."[34]

The Killer All Around Us

The Paris-based Organisation for Economic Co-operation and Development (OECD) isn't known for being the most radical of groups. A confederation of thirty-four of the wealthiest nations on the planet, it's based mainly around free markets and international trade. But at a conference in Leipzig, Germany, the OECD's secretary-general made a fairly startling remark about transport and equality.

"Right now, drivers pay to enjoy mobility," said Angel Gurría, a Mexican economist. "But the cost to the environment and to people's health isn't fully reflected in the price we pay to drive."[35] If you're a motorist, this might sound like pretty radical stuff: driving, worldwide, needs to be disincentivized by being made more expensive. But Gurría was absolutely right. He was talking about the global blight of vehicle-related pollution.

It's an indicator of the sheer, unimaginable human toll from the global dominance of motorized transport that even this third-most-lethal side effect—after physical inactivity and crashes—possibly kills about a million people a year around the world. When I say "possibly," that's not me fudging the facts. It's just that even the experts don't really know.

The World Health Organization (WHO) estimates that about 3.7 million people a year die early from outdoor air pollution—but this includes all sources, including industry, power stations, and smog from people burning domestic fuels.[36] These all mingle together, along with pollutants blown in from other countries, and separating the individual health hazards is difficult. One 2012 study from the UK, however, estimated that emissions from road transport contributes to about 40 percent of air pollution deaths.[37]

Much of this is due to especially fine particles, known technically as PM2.5s, as they're smaller than 2.5 micrometers, or 0.00025cm. These are the exhaust nasties that really affect people's health, proving especially deadly to children, the young, or those with existing heart or lung conditions. According to Dr. Gary Fuller, an expert on air quality at King's College (part of the University of London), about a quarter of PM2.5-related air pollution deaths in a big city might be caused by vehicle smog. You also need to factor in nitrogen dioxide, the pollutant at the center of the Volkswagen emissions test-fixing scandal, which affects people in a similar way.[38]

Nitrogen dioxide is, Fuller says, "the game changer for this type of calculation," given that even now the WHO is trying to calculate how many deaths it causes. However, he predicts, this work could double pollution mortality estimates. So, all in all, saying "a million people a year" is probably an underestimate.

Around half of all pollution-related deaths worldwide take place in India and China. WHO data shows India now has sixteen of the world's thirty cities with the highest concentrations of PM2.5s.[39] China, which has improved slightly in recent years, had five. As with traffic deaths, poorer nations see a predominance of pollution problems despite owning fewer vehicles overall. The same pattern also exists within cities. In Delhi, perhaps the most polluted major city in the world, census figures show just 21 percent of households own a motor vehicle.[40]

Similar inequalities over pollution exist even in richer countries. In 2002, a pair of academics from the University of Leeds undertook what they believed was the first UK study of the "potential environmental injustice" of vehicle smog. Their findings were striking. "The communities that have access to fewest cars tend to suffer from the highest levels of air pollution, whereas those in which car ownership is greatest enjoy the cleanest air," they wrote. "Pollution is most concentrated in areas where young children and their parents are more likely to live. Those communities that are most polluted and which also emit the least pollution tend to be amongst the poorest in Britain."[41]

Little has changed. In 2013, the Greater London Authority commissioned (but did not initially publish) a report into pollution around schools. It found that European Union limits for nitrogen dioxide levels were exceeded outside 433 junior schools. Of these, 83 percent were in economically deprived areas.[42]

Cyclists, of course, similarly emit no fumes but are on the front line of breathing them, something that, as an asthmatic, I take fairly personally. The one slightly good bit of news is that there is some evidence that being on a bike exposes you to lower levels of pollutants than you might think. In 2014, one of Gary Fuller's colleagues at King's College, Ben Barratt, attached instruments measuring exposure to black carbon, yet another pollutant associated with diesel fumes, to an ambulance driver, a cycle messenger, a young child, a retired person, an office worker, and a school student. They were also given GPS trackers and sent off for the same twenty-four-hour period. The cycle messenger ended up with the second-lowest reading of the group. Barratt said the ventilation from riding a bike might dissipate fumes, which tend to concentrate in a vehicle—the ambulance driver saw the highest exposure levels. There is also an argument that in congested cities, cycling can be quicker and allows you to use smaller side streets, further limiting your smog exposure.[43]

Sadly, there's a compensating factor—on a bike you tend to breathe more heavily, and thus ingest a greater proportion of what you're exposed to. This high respiration rate means that, overall, cyclists tend to absorb more pollutants than drivers, according to Dr. Audrey de Nazelle, an expert in air pollution at Imperial College London. However, she stresses, the benefits of physical activity still massively outweigh the risks, barring "very extreme conditions" such as cycling for a long period on a smoggy day in somewhere like Delhi.

The obvious point is that if you replace many thousands of car journeys in a city with bike trips, pollution levels fall. Some cities have begun to take emergency action to reduce smog. For example, Paris introduced emergency antismog rules to allow only cars with odd or even car registration numbers on alternate days, and now has a monthly ban on all cars in parts of the center. One of the first actions of London's new mayor, Sadiq Khan, upon being elected was to double the size of a zone within which particularly polluting vehicles must pay a charge, calling the city's air "our biggest environmental challenge."[44]

De Nazelle believes the urgency of the air pollution crisis makes it inevitable that others will follow. "I'm convinced that years from now we're going to look back at our age and think, wow, what were these people thinking?" she says. "We're going to look like we were living in Neanderthal conditions. It's not acceptable that we're exposed to the fumes we're living in right now. People are starting to recognize this."[45]

Saving the World

So far we've looked at how more cycling can improve equality connected to gender, age, culture, and income disparities, and the terrible death toll from vehicle pollution. But there's yet another social justice benefit that could arguably be seen as bigger than all these combined: helping to save the planet.

Global warming is too big, nuanced, and contentious an issue to cover comprehensively in one section of a single chapter of a general interest book about cycling. When the Intergovernmental Panel on Climate Change published its last report, the summary alone ran to sixty pages. But the importance of the issue is almost beyond overstatement. And, yet again, those currently suffering most acutely from the effects of a changing climate are, in general, those contributing least to the process. It's places like the Philippines, Ban-

gladesh, and the Maldives, which emit tiny amounts of greenhouse gases per head of population compared to industrialized
countries, but are bearing the brunt of ever-more-powerful
typhoons and rising sea levels. For example, per capita greenhouse gas emissions in the Philippines are about 5 percent of
what the average American produces,[46] and yet the country
has faced five of its ten most powerful typhoons in the
postwar era since 2006.[47]

What can cycling do? It's not going to change everything.
But a surprising amount of good would happen if, overnight,
every government in the world decided to build lots of bike
lanes.

A major study from 2011 by the European Cyclists' Federation (ECF) began by trying to compare average emissions
for bikes and e-bikes with other forms of transport, taking in
both the environmental cost of manufacture and of use,
which for bikes included extra calories consumed by the
rider. Even after factoring in a hefty average bike weight of
nearly almost forty-five pounds, the ECF calculated emissions of twenty-one grams of CO2e (carbon dioxide equivalent) per kilometer, with e-bikes putting out just one gram
more. In contrast, the emissions for a car were 271g/km per
person, with 101g/km per bus passenger.[48]

The study worked out that if every EU nation reached
Danish cycling levels, this would on its own make up between
5 percent and 11 percent of the emissions reductions needed
to reach the bloc's official 2020 emissions targets, and would
be between 57 percent and 125 percent of the reduction
needed in transport emissions.

A separate US report in 2015 worked out that e-bikes can often be more energy efficient per passenger kilometer than many rail systems. If the global share of urban journeys made by bike even rose slightly from the current 6 percent or so to 11 percent in 2030 and 14 percent in 2050, this would cut overall emissions by 7 percent (in 2030) and then 11 percent (in 2050).[49]

As mentioned at the start of the chapter, it's long been a cliché among noncyclists that those who ride a bike are puritan environmental zealots who choose their clunky, antiquated mode of transport out of a hair-shirt desire to rescue the planet. They might be wrong about the motivation, but it seems we're helping to do so nonetheless.

On Equal Terms

It may seem a rhetorical stretch to argue that the same types of attitudes that deny a choice of cheap, independent mobility to the most vulnerable of transport users—the young, the old, the poor, or people with disabilities—are also destroying the planet. It's ultimately a matter of opinion. But what does seem clear is that policies that open up cycling as a realistic transportation choice to as many people as possible end up having significant, and not always entirely intended, positive effects.

Let's end by considering a city in which transportation is more open and accessible. This winter I returned to Copenhagen for the first time since I left it at age twelve. I spent a couple of January days cycling around the city with my son, then age five: me pedaling a weighty rented cargo bike, him wrapped up in a pair of thick blankets in the front section. Progress was slow, the light was dim, and there were occasional snow flurries. But, as when I was riding around as a ten-year-old, not once did I feel concerned.

Things are, of course, more complex than they appear. We went to see Klaus Bondam at the headquarters of the Cyklistforbundet, Denmark's main cycling group, which he leads. Bondam recounted a recent Facebook post that had gone viral in the city. Written by the mother of a six-year-old girl, it was addressed to Copenhagen's adult cyclists. *Please,* she wrote, *do not overtake my daughter so closely, and at speed, or ring your bell, as she cycles to school. She's six. She sometimes wobbles. Be patient.*

Bondam explained that space on Copenhagen's bike lanes is becoming increasingly tight amid ever greater numbers of cyclists, which can bring conflict. "I would be lying if I said there were no tensions," he said. "You do get children, and old people, who are passed too close. And we have to work this out. It's a huge challenge."[50]

But these are difficulties, not a structural, institutional acceptance of limited mobility. We later visited Morten Kabell, Copenhagen's mayor for transport and infrastructure (the city council has a series of mayors with varying responsibilities). As we sat in his airy office inside the city hall, my son playing with a Lego set under the desk (Danes are generally very relaxed about children), Kabell explained how he approaches his task of helping an increasingly big and varied population make their various ways around the city.

"It's about livability," he said. "People joke that I'm the least people-oriented of the mayors. I don't have responsibility for any teachers, or nurses. And in many ways this is a technical area. But actually what we're doing is the most people-oriented, because this is the basis of how everybody is living their lives.

"Here—unlike with things like social care and health care—here we meet Copenhageners on equal terms. An eighty-year-old woman who prefers to walk, or a fit twenty-five-year-old guy cycling from his university—they're met on equal terms. They're both Copenhageners who we need to take care of and make sure they have mobility."[51]

CHAPTER 4

A Happier, More Prosperous World

We Try to Think About a Good Life

Directly opposite Odense's Italianate nineteenth-century city hall sits a squat and considerably less elegant temporary boxlike structure, dropped amid a mass of ongoing construction work. This is an information bureau for people to learn more about the huge reconstruction project transforming Denmark's third-biggest city. Inside, the centerpiece is an enormous, carved-wood scale model of the city center, with every street and building. But show this to an observant local and they might soon spot a few differences.

In the world outside, just north of here, runs Thomas B. Thrige Street, named after a businessman who founded a firm making electric motors in 1890s—part of an industrial boom which transformed Odense into the manufacturing center of Denmark. The street carrying his name was built in the early 1960s and is typical of the urban freeways of that era—a rapid, four-lane route built across what was the old city. But on the wooden model, Thomas B. Thrige Street looks very different. The cars are gone. It is now a tree-filled route for pedestrians and cyclists, lined by new cafés, shops, and apartments.

This is part of a radical and locally controversial plan to more or less banish cars from the city center. Anker Boye, Odense's veteran mayor—a somewhat unconventional politician who began his working life as a house painter—describes the rationale behind the $4 billion plan, which will be completed in 2020. Yes, he says, encouraging more people to cycle and walk will bring the usual improvements to public health, pollution, and the like. But the primary motivation is something less immediately obvious: keeping Odense, a small and relatively obscure city in international terms, economically competitive in the globalized world.

"In this little country we are one of the big cities, and for generations we were the industrial center," Boye says. "But that has all changed. In the global market we're small. So we're concentrating on the clever parts of industrialization, like technology."

These new industries include a European center for testing drones and medical research connected to the city's university. The mayor's bet for the future is that with heavy industry now more or less gone—Odense's shipyard building huge container vessels finally closed in 2012—there is no longer an economic need for mass road capacity to carry trucks and cars. The newer, high-tech firms, he hopes, will be drawn to the city more for its quality of life, particularly lots of green spaces and safe cycling.

"We no longer need all the cars in the city center," Boye says. "More and more investors are coming here, because they believe in the way we've transformed this old, industrial city into a new city. We try to think about people living here all their life, and having a good life here."[1]

By the standards of most places, Odense is already very welcoming to bikes. With just under two hundred thousand people, it has almost 350 miles of bike lanes and 123 cyclist-only bridges.[2] But Boye and his colleagues say they need to exploit this advantage to the full. The rebuilt city center will see drivers obliged to head to either underground parking garages or park-and-ride systems. A lot of people, the designers hope, will choose instead to cycle or use a new tramline.

Boye says the focus is also on adding cultural centers and cafés, and ensuring enough of the new housing is affordable for people on lower incomes. "We know we need to live from private businesses, so we need to have good conditions for that," he says. "But we care about the whole life of people. It's many things together."

Odense epitomizes a relatively recent shift in the way people think about urban cycling. For a long time, bike advocates tended to be from the political left, from green movements, or both. But in the last decade a new set of arguments has emerged that contend that building better bike infrastructure is as much about boosting the local economy. This is billed as a new model for competitive cities—that they are these days judged less on busy roads than people-friendly streets lined with pavement cafés. It is, however, about more than just ever-rising GDP figures. As with Odense, this philosophy aims to bring about a happier, healthier, more human-scale city. And at the heart of these changes is cycling.

The high priest of this doctrine, you won't be too surprised to know, is another Dane.

Jan Gehl, now in his eighties, is an architect and urban planner who is best known for his ideas about livable cities. Gehl argues that people are happiest when they are able to engage with their surroundings on a human level. City dwellers, Gehl argues, should feel "they are invited to walk as much as possible and to bicycle as much as possible."

I met Gehl when he was on a visit to London in 2013. At the time, the city had yet to build much in the way of safe cycling infrastructure, and Gehl was visibly less than impressed by a local bike culture he described as "for the extreme sport enthusiasts, the freaks who think, 'It's a good day if I survive.'"

London, he argued forcefully to me, was being left behind in the "new set of paradigms" on which cities were judged. "In the past they competed on who had the most parking spaces, or the biggest freeways, or the highest skyscrapers," he said. "But now there are many more questions about quality of life and livability."

There are, Gehl noted, three well-respected annual lists of the world's most livable cities, each with dozens of places on them. No UK city features anywhere. "As far as I'm concerned, that's because you have a very, very strong tradition of letting the traffic planners rule," he said. "They are still in a very strong position. They think that what you see out here is given by God. It's not. We are realizing that if you have people walk and bicycle more, you have a more lively, more livable, more attractive, more safe, more sustainable, and more healthy city. And what are you waiting for?"[3]

We Do Not Want to Lose Any More

So what was London waiting for? In part, it was waiting for the then-mayor, Boris Johnson, to stop building bike lanes marked only by paint, and embark on a network of better-designed cycle routes. This he did, and fairly soon: work began on the city's first major separated lanes in early 2014. The complex and fascinating political battle behind this process is told in chapter 6, but one element in particular illustrates the changing attitude of big business to mass cycling.

The two lanes were fairly modest by most standards, one running a few miles north to south across the city center, and another longer lane bisecting it east to west. But this was a politically charged moment. It was the first time a mayor in the city had definitively taken small if noticeable chunks of space from motor vehicles and given them to bikes, and some groups were not happy at all.

The opposition was relatively small, but extremely noisy and quite influential, including the trade organization representing London's famous black taxis. Equally outraged were some members of parliament, whose regular drive to work was delayed for a period by the construction of the east–west route. As well as being the mayor, Johnson was also a member of parliament. Some of his fellow MPs would harangue him on a virtually daily basis about the inconvenience, he said later.

The volume of complaints rose ever higher, and all conveyed the same message: such bike lanes were bad for business. They might be okay in a Utrecht or an Odense, but London was a global city and relied on the free road movement of deliveries and people. The city would grind to a halt.

Then a slightly surprising voice emerged in favor of Johnson's plans. Dozens of companies, among them corporate behemoths like Microsoft, Coca-Cola, the bank Santander, mobile phone firm Vodafone, and Tesco (the UK's biggest supermarket chain) combined to form a lobby group called CyclingWorks. This argued that new bike infrastructure in London was utterly necessary for the efficiency of the companies. There was another reason, they said: all their staff had a right to expect to get to work safely, however they traveled.

"We have tragically lost employees in the past who have been killed while trying to cycle to or from work," wrote Unilever, the Anglo-Dutch household goods multinational. "We do not want to lose any more. Our sister head office building in Rotterdam is surrounded by cycle lanes and an efficient urban tramway system. We see the benefits to urban mobility and quality of life."[4]

Not all businesses signed up. One major property group secretly paid for the taxi drivers' union to make an expensive and doomed legal challenge to the bike lanes. It later emerged that the company's main concern was that visiting executives would face longer limousine journeys to and from the airport.[5]

Speaking to me as he officially unveiled one of the new lanes just before his mayoral term ended in May 2016, Johnson said CyclingWorks had been an important movement. "I think there's been a big change in London, and London businesses increasingly understand this," he said. "One of the reassuring things about this whole exercise is that, even though we got very heavily attacked, businesses all the way along the route have pretty much all supported it."[6]

It's worth noting that Johnson, while a politically brave supporter of cycling facilities, is a Conservative, and by no means a champion of wider questions of equality and environmental change. During his eight years in office, air quality in London deteriorated,[7] while a laissez-faire attitude to property speculation contributed to massive social changes in many neighborhoods. Similarly, it's hard to argue that companies like Coca-Cola and Tesco have an all-pervading interest in public health, let alone a commitment to social justice. But their interest in cycling as an economic force, or even just something they should be seen to support, is nonetheless fascinating. There are still those in big business who argue that a vibrant and competitive city is based around roads choked with cars, taxis, and vans. But they are increasingly starting to look like dinosaurs, clinging to a bygone era.

Rewriting the Code of the Streets

Boris Johnson was not the only mayor of a major global city to recently push through new cycling infrastructure amid noisy opposition, despite holding avowedly free-market opinions.

Michael Bloomberg, former mayor of New York City, predated Johnson in becoming serious about cycling, and was something of an inspiration to his London counterpart. While in many ways an unusual (not to mention late-joining) Republican, with his sidelines in philanthropy and environmental issues, New York's mayor from 2002–13 is arguably even more a devotee of unfettered, unregulated economics than Johnson—he is a multibillionaire entrepreneur who nonetheless vetoed a "living wage" bill to give some local workers a statutory pay increase.[8]

It's also fair to say Bloomberg is probably not a sentimentalist about cycling, the type to wax about the pleasure of feeling the wind in your hair. His vision for bikes was rational, a direct response of his awkwardly named PlaNYC, a 2007 document that sought to prepare the city for the expected arrival of another million residents in the coming years.

Bloomberg's commissioner for transport and, for good or ill, the public face of the city's new bike lanes and associated car-free public plazas, was Janette Sadik-Khan. While a technocrat rather than a politician, Sadik-Khan talks in similarly free market ways about the city's previous overreliance on the car and how this meant it was "getting diminishing returns" from its infrastructure.

"Transportation is not an ideology, it's not a left or right thing," she told me. "It's about taking a look at the capital asset we have and using it in the most effective way possible. For so long the way we measured transportation, the way we measured our streets, had been about the flow of traffic, how fast was traffic going, which ignores all the other ways a street is used.

"The future of our cities depends on the decisions that we make today. These changes are not amenities, they're investments. It's not about a crunchy, green, granola approach to our streets, it's about economic development strategy for cities."

The mission, Sadik-Khan said, is to "rewrite the operating code of the street," or more specifically, "put a hole in the myth that more lanes and more parking spaces are better for business."[9]

It is a curiously enduring myth, the idea that businesses can thrive only with free-flowing cars and easy, cheap parking. One factor seems to be that business owners continually overestimate how many of their customers drive to reach them. One much-cited study from Graz in Austria asked shopkeepers to estimate what proportion of customers arrived in a car. They guessed 58 percent, when the real figure was about half that.[10] Studies from places including Copenhagen have shown that while shoppers on a bike will tend to purchase less per trip than those in a car, they visit more often, and so tend on average to spend more overall.[11]

All this, you might argue, is all very well in a Graz or a Copenhagen, but what about really big cities?

New York is a fascinating example here. When the city started to earmark certain streets for the first protected bike lanes and car-free plazas, some shops and other businesses along the routes complained vociferously. How would customers get to them? they asked. They claimed it would be disastrous for trade. They were completely wrong.

In 2013, the city's transport department commissioned a series of detailed studies about the impact on businesses along some of the city's new bike routes, and the findings were striking. The researchers discovered that by the third year of a protected bike lane on Ninth Avenue in Manhattan, business revenues there had risen 49 percent, against 26 percent along a trio of comparable streets without bike routes. The picture was similar in Brooklyn, where a cycle route on Vanderbilt Avenue near Prospect Park saw sales double over three years, compared to a local average of about 60 percent. This was a pattern repeated almost wherever the researchers looked.

"It is clear that rolling out safer, more inviting and sustainable streets is rarely detrimental to local businesses and in the great majority of cases can be a boon to them," the report concluded. The research, it added with some justified smugness, "offers a significant contribution in the US and around the world to the advancement of a 21st-century approach to urban street design."[12]

Thanks in part to research like this, the pro-business case for more cycling has become increasingly well known in recent years. This is, however, only half of the argument.

What is less commonly appreciated is the huge and often un-noticed damage to an economy when roads are dominated by motor vehicles. Too many cars are very much bad for business.

Everything You Know About Parking Is Wrong

"My father never paid for parking, my mother, my brother, nobody," says George Costanza in one episode of the New York City–based sitcom *Seinfeld*. "It's like going to a prostitute. Why should I pay when, if I apply myself, maybe I could get it for free?"

This quote is used in a *New York Times* article[13] by Donald Shoup, a professor of urban planning at UCLA. Shoup has devoted much of his career to a single subject, penning two dozen papers on it as well as an eight-hundred-page book, described by its publisher as a "no-holds-barred treatise." The subject? Yes, parking.

Parking, especially free, on-street parking, is one of those areas that many people seem somehow to take both entirely for granted and very, very personally. People in New York seem to "treat every parking space like it was their firstborn child," says Janette Sadik-Khan, recalling the battles she endured over it. Her near-equivalent, Andrew Gilligan, Boris Johnson's mayoral commissioner for cycling in London from 2013 to 2015, once confessed he never even tried to properly tackle the subject. "Parking is the third rail of politics," he said, referring to the live power line that runs between the tracks of many subway systems. "If you touch it, you die."[14]

If any thought is given to the economics of easy on-street parking, the assumption is often that its impact is generally neutral. Some spaces are paid for, and even the free ones contribute by assisting a constant shuffle of consumers. Shoup disagrees. He sees it as a vast waste of resources, pointing to research showing that in Manhattan, almost a third of drivers at any one time are looking for on-street parking, a figure that rises to 45 percent in Brooklyn.[15]

A study by Shoup and his students around a fifteen-block area of Los Angeles found the average person drove half a mile looking for parking, making for a combined annual 950,000 wasted vehicle miles in just that area. "If all this happens in one small business district, imagine the cumulative effect of all cruising in the United States," he wrote.[16]

Shoup's anger is also directed at free off-street parking lots, calling them a huge subsidy to the generally richer population of car owners. He estimated that in twelve US cities, the average construction cost for an aboveground parking space is $24,000, almost four times the median net worth for black households.[17] Overall, he has calculated, such free parking amounts to a subsidy of about $500 billion a year, meaning that for every dollar a motorist spends directly on their car, there is a fifty-cent cost connected to parking that is met by others.[18]

The idea of car use being subsidized by such a sum might seem shocking. But it's just one of the hidden costs imposed on society at large by car use. Calculating the figure for these costs, known as externalities, is a fascinating if occasionally opaque process, one open to endless debate and estimates. A

2012 study by German academics worked out that just road crashes, pollution, and noise from cars cost $420 billion a year across the EU, or about $850 per man, woman, and child, much more than was raised in motoring-related taxes.[19]

The most exhaustive, almost borderline-obsessive, chronicling of the hidden costs of cars has been carried out by the Victoria Transport Policy Institute, an independent research organization based in the Canadian city of that name.

It's an extremely dense report on the issue that runs to five hundred pages, and covers all sorts of costs, many of which might well have never occurred to you. A few are borne just by vehicle owners, such as running costs and travel time. But the list of externalities is longer, including safety, parking, congestion, the construction of roads, the land value of roads, traffic law enforcement, air and water pollution, noise, resource use, and the disposal of car-based waste like old batteries and tires.

Altogether, the institute concludes, people who are not car owners pay about 35 percent of the total costs of vehicle use, or anything from twenty-seven cents to fifty-five cents per mile driven. For the United States, this totals $1.15 trillion a year in externalities. If you add together internal and external costs, the study concludes, it amounts to about 25 percent of American GDP.[20]

Of course, vehicle use doesn't only impose costs on an economy. Trucks do move vital goods, every minute of every day. Cars get millions of people to and from work. The main problem is that the economic efficiency of a car-dominated transport system is often wildly overstated, especially for cities.

Why You're Driving More Slowly Than You Think

Part of this excessive belief in the economic efficiency of the motor vehicle is based around one area that many people have most likely never considered: their car almost certainly travels much more slowly than they think.

This can be a strange notion to introduce. But fear not, I'm not about to describe some shadowy global conspiracy. This isn't about actual speed, as shown on the dashboard. This is the concept known as effective speed.

"Effective speed" means, in its simplest form, considering a vehicle's speed as also being a factor of its cost, and thus how long we need to work to pay for it. Paul Tranter, an academic at the University of New South Wales in Australia, uses the analogy of someone living in a village who spends an hour a day fetching water on foot. Imagine they could construct a clockwork machine to get the water for them, but it needed to be wound up for an hour every morning. Would they take this into account when deciding if the machine was worthwhile? Of course they would.

Tranter argues that the modern equivalent of this is the time people spend earning the money needed to pay for a form of transport. And you need to spend a lot more time at work to pay for a car and its running costs than those of a bike.

He has calculated effective speeds for a hypothetical cyclist and the owners of various cars living in Canberra, Australia's capital city, a place deliberately chosen to the advantage of cars with its generally free-flowing roads. Even here, Tranter calculates, the effective cycling speed of 11.3 mph is quicker than any but the cheapest car. The tiny and now defunct Hyundai Getz managed 14.4 mph, although for younger drivers the higher insurance premiums dropped this to 9.3 mph.

In contrast was the Holden Monaro, with its 5.7 liter V8 engine and top speed of 150 mph, which was so expensive to run it had an effective speed of just 9.1 mph.[21]

This can seem a bit like a theoretical game, and of limited use to the real world. But it's worthwhile for two reasons. The first is individual. Studies have shown that people consistently underestimate the cost of driving and overestimate how much they need to pay for public transport. It's thus a worthwhile exercise to show how using a car is often a far worse economic deal than generally billed, especially in a city, so people can make an economically rational choice if they want.

I spent a fair few years as a car owner in London, figuring that once bought, the vehicle was a reasonably good deal, even for the very occasional use it got. But the moment I totted up a year's combined bills for fuel, insurance, parking, and servicing and repairs, even driving a couple thousand miles a year came to the same cost as buying a pretty expensive bike.

The other use comes when politicians discuss the economic benefit of building new roads, based on the idea they will cut journey times. But as Tranter notes, even if a new road made it somehow possible to double average in-car speeds—which is very unlikely in itself—their effective speed would remain almost unchanged.

Tranter stresses he is by no means the first person to think of travel in this way. He quotes the US writer and thinker Henry David Thoreau, who in his 1854 book *Walden* described the varying merits of getting to the next town on foot or by train.

"I start now on foot, and get there before night," Thoreau wrote. "You will in the meanwhile have earned your fare, and arrive there some time tomorrow, or possibly this evening, if you are lucky enough to get a job in season. Instead of going to Fitchburg, you will be working here the greater part of the day. And so, if the railroad reached round the world, I think that I should keep ahead of you."

How More Cycling Means More Friends

The economic argument might seem pretty comprehensive, especially when it comes to encouraging more cycling in towns and cities. But, if you remember, the aim for Odense in almost ridding its city center of cars is not just to become more rich, but for its people to have a better life. This is where the arguments get more personal.

I'm as convinced as I can be that cycling makes me happier. On the occasional days I take the train to work, I generally arrive much as I left home—slightly fuzzy-headed and not yet fully engaged with the day. When I cycle, I get to the office not just physically invigorated but more cheery, with a greater sense of mental balance and well-being.

In part this is just the magical effect of exercise. The mood-lifting role of endorphins, released by physical exertion, is very well-known these days, and a fairly central element of many treatments for depression. With cycling, there is something else. It's the personal element. On a bike you're very clearly a human, and other humans can interact with you. Scientists estimate that people's ability to make proper eye contact with someone else becomes impossible at speeds beyond about 20 mph, above which few urban cyclists travel.[22] It's one of the many reasons why motor vehicles tend to be an impersonal, cut-off way to get about. And it helps explain why cycling doesn't only improve the happiness of the people who do it. It can have a transformative effect on the communities they live in.

Donald Appleyard was an English urban designer who spent his academic life teaching and researching in the United States. He is best known for *Livable Streets*, a 1969 study and later book, which created considerable publicity at the time. At the center of this was an in-depth comparison of three residential streets in San Francisco which were broadly similar but for levels of motor traffic.

One, which saw about two thousand vehicles pass along it a day, was referred to in the book as Light Street. Medium Street saw eight thousand vehicles a day, with sixteen thousand on Heavy Street. Appleyard found that Light Street was viewed by locals as a close-knit community, in which people's "territory"—the area they saw as their own—encompassed the entire road. People would stand on the sidewalk or on the front steps of homes to chat; children would play.

In contrast, Heavy Street saw very little sense of community, with people mainly using it as a conduit to go from their home to somewhere else. Appleyard found that on average, people living on Light Street had three times more friends and twice as many acquaintances among their neighbors as those on Heavy Street. As the volume of traffic increased, he found, people's perceived territory shrank.[23]

Appleyard's opportunity to further his research was cut short: in 1982, the year after the book of his studies was published, he was struck and killed by the driver of a speeding car in Athens, Greece, at age fifty-four.

However, later studies have reinforced the findings. Research from 2008 in Bristol, a city in the west of England, focused on three otherwise similar streets with an even greater variance in traffic, ranging from about 140 vehicles a day to 21,000. Again, the contrasts were stark. People on the lightest-trafficked road reported a sense of community. In contrast, a man living on the busiest street described twenty-one thousand vehicles a day as a "mountain range, cutting you off from the other side of the road." Those on the quietest road had more than twice as many acquaintances and five times as many friends than did those on the road with the most traffic.[24]

It's no surprise that homes on car-dominated roads tend to be considerably cheaper to buy or rent than those on more quiet thoroughfares. Again, as we saw in the last chapter, this is the population of car owners disproportionately visiting the social costs of their transport habit onto poorer people. And these costs can be very high. Studies have shown social isolation correlates with poorer mental and physical health.[25] A lack of social support has even been demonstrated to increase the chance of dying prematurely.[26]

Perhaps the world's leading expert on what makes people happy is Professor John Helliwell, a Canadian academic who coedits the UN's annual World Happiness Report. He is very clear about one key reason behind contentment: "The single biggest factor is the extent to which people think their neighbors can be trusted. Neighborhoods that work, in the sense of producing trusting neighbors, are ones where they spend a lot of time with each other, thinking about each other and doing things with each other. In places where that's natural or easier to achieve, it happens more readily."[27]

Tourism by the Centimeter

For the best description I've ever heard about the happiness-inducing impact of riding a bike, let me introduce you to Cesare. When he was eighty-three, he was interviewed as part of an entrancing and illuminating study in the journal *Medical Anthropology*. The wonderfully titled "The Bicycle Makes the Eyes Smile" saw a US academic, Elizabeth Whitaker, chronicle in depth the physical and mental well-being of a group of road cyclists in the north of Italy who, despite being between fifty-two and eighty-four, undertook rides up to fifty miles or more several times a week.

These were leisure cyclists, not commuters or people running chores, fetching shopping or children, and thus arguably a bit outside the scope of this book. They were also, as Whitaker concedes, "positive deviants" who exercised far more than most modern people, let alone those in older age. They were in fantastic physical condition, almost all of them with a body mass index well below the Italian average, which is in turn low by global standards. One of the men, eighty-three-year-old Alvaro, who went on fifty-mile rides two or three times a week, said his lungs remained so strong, "I could sing on the climbs."

It is, however, the mental and emotional impact of the cycling which is expressed so lyrically, and makes the study such a joy. "It makes you feel good, both physically and mentally. This is no small thing, to feel well with oneself," said Ernesto, sixty-one. Daniele, who was the same age but only started to ride at age fifty, expressed the sentiment that gives the paper its title, while seventy-five-year-old Giovanni merely said, "The bicycle gave me life."

And what of Cesare? He rode seven days a week, for only about ten miles at a time, albeit with three uphill sections. The retired teacher, now a painter and poet, is very likely my favorite subject in any academic research, ever. He boasted of never having had his blood pressure checked, as he only cares about the pressure in his bicycle tires. Of his cycling he said: "I do it because it is my passion, because it is a habit; it is a habit that attached itself affectionately to me."

Cesare told Whitaker he had ridden exactly the same route every day for several decades, saying this allowed him to fully see and appreciate the surroundings, which provide inspiration for his poems and pictures. He described the process as "tourism by the centimeter." Whitaker continues her portrait of Cesare: "He describes the things that animate the countryside for him: a rooster that crows every time he approaches; a daffodil he fell in love with for three months before it 'betrayed' him by dying; a pair of road signs in a ditch, which he saw as a male and female fallen in an eternal embrace. He says the route never bores him for he always sees it differently. And while he seems to live in an enchanted world, the cycling is of concrete value since, in fact, he paints many of the things he sees on his rides, including road signs."[28]

Most of us can but aspire to live in Cesare's enchanted world. But one thing seems clear: you're more likely to see it from the saddle of a bike than the seat of a car.

CHAPTER 5

Build It, and They Will Come

José Garcia Cebrián's moment of success came earlier than expected. The network of protected bike lanes for which he had battled to build for so many years in his home city were still under construction when cyclists started hopping over builders' barriers to use them.

"Sections had been laid, but they were far from done," says the man who, as Seville's head of urban planning, oversaw the installation of fifty miles of fully segregated cycleways in the southern Spanish city in 2006. "Some people were so keen they lifted their bikes over the fences and rode anyway. It was all okay, apart from a couple of people who did this at night and crashed into barriers where a section finished."

All this paled in comparison to the scene when the network was officially opened, recalls Cebrián, sipping a coffee at a café inside Seville's medieval city: "As soon as the work was finishing and the fences were removed the cyclists just came. The head of the building team, who'd been very skeptical about the process, called me and said, 'Where have all those cyclists come from?' That's when I knew for sure it was going to work. They came from all over the city."[1]

They continued to come. Within a couple of years of the lanes opening, along with other initiatives including a public bike-share system, the number of cycle trips in Seville multiplied elevenfold. This is, admittedly, from a tiny 0.5 percent starting point for trips made by bike.[2] The current level, just over 6 percent, is impressive, but nowhere near the standards of an equivalent Dutch or Danish city.

Seville's green-tarmacked bike network, now expanded to seventy-five miles, has its compromises. Riding around it with Manuel Calvo, the local urban designer hired by Cebrián to build the network, he happily points out the flaws. A lack of space given over for the lanes means they are not hugely wide for the two-way cycle traffic, and occasionally narrow to pinch points, or even feature the occasional tree. But the system feels coherent, connected, and, above all, safe, with cyclists separated from vehicle traffic by a curb, as well as often by a fence.

Seville is seen as a hugely significant example within the global debate over how you get more people cycling. For many years the skeptics' mantra to bike campaigners in places such as Spain—as well as the likes of the United States, the UK, and Australia—was that they were wasting their time. The Dutch and Danish had preexisting, decades-old cycle cultures, which could not just be magicked up with some cement and a few barriers.

Cebrián, Calvo, and their colleagues proved them wrong. They took a crowded, ancient city with no real history of cycling and summer temperatures that regularly go above 100 degrees Fahrenheit and decided to see what would happen if they just built some decent cycling infrastructure.

The effect, it seems, happens not just in terms of cyclist numbers, but also the wider cycling culture. On my guided tour with Calvo, the lanes were being well used, even outside rush hour. And while we saw riders of all ages and on all sorts of bikes, they had one thing in common: almost none wore helmets and just about everyone was dressed in ordinary clothes. Rather than "cyclists"—enthusiasts, hobbyists, campaigners—these were people who had gotten on bikes as the quickest, easiest way to move around.

Having turned Seville into an unlikely global poster city for modern cycling, Cebrián and Calvo now regularly escort fact-finding officials from foreign municipalities around their network. In fact, they note gloomily, the one place that has shown the least curiosity is their own country. "We've had more visitors from the rest of Europe looking at what we've done than we have had from Spain," said Calvo.

Seville's example is dramatic, but not unique. Just about everywhere that has built workable bike infrastructure has seen a resultant rush of cyclists. Conversely there is, virtually without exception, no city or country that has significant amounts of cycling that has not rebuilt its streets for bikes. I say "virtually" because of the anomaly of Japan. Tokyo, for example, has almost no on-road bike lanes, and yet about 15 percent of journeys are by bicycle.[3] This happens, however, because cyclists routinely use sidewalks instead. The cycling culture is utilitarian and gentle, with most people riding the ubiquitous mamachari, or granny bikes, usually laden with shopping, children, even an umbrella. It's a compromise that works there, but has never been successfully exported.

Everywhere else it is bike lanes that have proven to be the catalyst. New York City has seen a massive increase in cyclists since Mayor Michael Bloomberg's conversion to cycle lanes in 2006. Levels were creeping up anyway, rising about 70 percent between 2000 and 2006. But from 2006 to 2014, they shot up 250 percent.[4]

In London, the first snippet of proper separated routing, around the previously fearsome Vauxhall gyratory just south of the River Thames, saw bike numbers increase 75 percent in just four months.[5]

Even better things were to come. As we heard in the introduction, when London's first major separated routes were completed, within just over a month, cyclist numbers were 60 percent higher.[6] Andrew Gilligan, London's then-commissioner for cycling, recalls Seville-like scenes while the new lanes were being constructed, with riders using each completed yard of the "superhighways" more or less as soon as the asphalt had dried. "They were breaking through the barriers when the thing wasn't even ready," he says. "They wanted to ride on it so badly."[7]

If you get a chance to use one of the new lanes you can see

why. Like in Seville, they're two-way, but wide, smooth and with all the extra safety features you'd hope for, like cyclist-only traffic lights to stop vehicles turning across bikes. What I notice most as I move from the bus and truck frenzy of the preceding street to one of the lanes is a sense of my body un-tensing slightly. It is cycling as a relaxing pleasure, not an invigorating thrill.

This is one of the oddly fascinating things about infrastructure. It's not the most alluring of words, reminiscent of power lines and sewage plants. But traffic infrastructure has a huge capacity to shape the way people move about and live, especially in a city. Wherever there are people on the move, much of the way they interact is shaped by the planned environment for different types of transport.

And when it comes to roads, these interactions are far from equal. Speeding traffic intimidates pedestrians, as it does anyone not caged and cocooned inside a tin box. The most unequal interaction of all, arguably, is between cyclists and the vehicles with which, in far too many towns and cities, they are obliged to share space. If you decide that this relationship is essentially okay—and this, often by default, is what has been decided in the bulk of towns and cities globally—then you can forget about having more than a few percent of your population deciding to ride a bike.

This is deeply unfair. Global experience over the decades has shown that if mixing with the motor traffic is your chosen bike environment, then almost all your cyclists will be a small group who are mainly young, predominantly male, and disproportionately gung ho.

Often this discussion becomes reduced to talk of various

types of bike lanes. As we'll see below, to create mass cycling you need to shape the built environment in several other ways, too. And for all the occasionally opaque discussions about curb heights, lane barriers, and traffic light phases, this is about something more fundamental. Bike infrastructure is, at its heart, about a changed vision for the place occupied by human beings in the modern urban world.

Cars Are Guests

To examine how all this can work in practice, I went to Houten, a new town of about fifty thousand people just south of Utrecht in the central Netherlands. While generally little known overseas, Houten is a remarkable place in a couple of ways. To begin, as with all artificially created communities, its center has a strange uniformity of architecture, in this case a style that could be called Early Eighties Redbrick Municipal. But then you notice something else. For anyone used to the constant if barely noticed road hum of most towns and cities, it feels oddly quiet. "It's not for everyone," admits Martijn van Es, the affable press officer for the Dutch Cyclists' Union, the Fietsersbond, who has taken me on a bike tour to Houten. "The people who live here say it's the best place in the world. Personally I prefer a bit more excitement."[8]

Houten is at the more radical end of Dutch planning for bikes, itself generally seen as the best there is. An existing village around which a new community was planned and built from 1978, architect Rob Derks's design was based on a traffic system that sees cars largely exiled to outer ring roads, from which they can then creep down a few streets at no more than 15 mph. In contrast, Houten's center is criss-crossed with eighty miles of red-paved bike paths, which are not only completely safe but offer by far the most convenient route for people to get almost anywhere.

The results are quite something. Houten's train station has indoor parking for about three thousand bikes,[9] with steps leading straight up to the platforms. It is almost always full. Cars are far from unknown, with ownership levels just slightly below the Dutch national average. But they are more or less banished from the center. Surveys show that if locals are visiting friends or running errands rather than doing the weekly grocery shopping, something close to 70 percent of them choose to use their bikes.[10]

All that said, for me the most remarkable element of my trip to Houten was how we got there. Van Es took me from the Fietsersbond headquarters in central Utrecht via a fairly circuitous route (in part as we got lost a couple of times) along urban streets, through the university district, and down semirural lanes. None of this was a preplanned cycling utopia like Houten, simply the everyday Dutch road environment— one retrofitted over the decades so more or less anyone can feel safe and comfortable. For someone used to London it was a huge pleasure and at the time very slightly depressing— all my bike trips could and should be more like this. For about three-quarters of the route we were on separated bike lanes or traffic-free paths. Where we shared space with cars, they approached us cautiously and overtook with care. Inside

Utrecht, some streets were officially designated as "cycling streets." These had prominent signs showing the silhouette of a cyclist ahead of a vehicle with the message "auto te gast": "Cars are guests."

When we returned to the Fietsersbond office I remarked to the organization's director, Saskia Kluit, how unstressful the whole experience had been compared to my normal London riding. "It's not a miracle," she said. "It's just years of hard work. We started in the nineteen seventies here, and you started in the nineteen nineties. So you have another twenty years to go. But then you learn from us, and you don't have to make the mistakes we did."

To repeat: it's not a miracle. Also, it's not just cultural. And it's not because the Netherlands and Denmark are flat, or have temperate weather. These are all the case. But ultimately it's about choices. This can't be emphasized enough.

If another nation suddenly decided it wanted to follow the Dutch or Danish model, then the changes would take time. But the only other real obstacle would be political and public will. How you do it is very well known. The practicalities have been refined and proven in the decades since both countries decided they wanted to reverse the postwar trend for car-dominated streets. A series of towns and cities in other nations have tried very similar things and, more or less without exception, they have also seen success, too. So what's the secret?

At the most basic level there are a few main principles,

with a handful of other associated tenets. First is the idea that, wherever possible, bikes should be kept separate from motor traffic on busy roads. "Busy" can be a matter of interpretation, but should encompass more or less any main route.

The Dutch bike infrastructure bible *Design Manual for Bicycle Traffic,* produced by the traffic organization CROW, recommends physical segregation on any route where the traffic flow is greater than a far-from-huge two thousand motor vehicles per day. The protection must be continuous, meaning at junctions bikes need a barrier, or their own phased traffic lights. If that seems too technical you can think about it in the more evocative phrase of Enrique Peñalosa, the bike lane–building mayor of Bogotá, who we met in chapter 3: "A bicycle way that is not safe for an eight-year-old is not a bicycle way." This means the routes are not only safe, but they are forgiving, obvious to use, and inspire confidence.

The separation must be physical. Lanes marked with just paint won't do it. In fact there's evidence that in some cases this can be worse than nothing. Perhaps the biggest such leap of faith was London's first generation of so-called Cycle Superhighways, launched amid some fanfare in 2010 as a network of quick commuting routes radiating out from the city center. These were delineated by just a bright blue strip, with nothing beyond the slight possibility of a traffic fine to keep cars and trucks out. This brought inevitable and very occasionally tragic results. A coroner examining the deaths of two cyclists on the routes warned that a painted lane could "lull riders into a false sense of security."[11]

After another fatality, my newspaper sent me out to make a

film, showing what it was like to ride the painted super-highway.[12] It was fairly basic—me giving a running commentary to the ride into a clip microphone while a series of GoPro action cameras strapped to me and the bike showed the scene—but the eventual footage of vans and trucks whizzing past and veering across me into the paint demarcation was eloquent. "You call that a bike lane?" e-mailed one viewer from the Netherlands. "That's not a bike lane. It's a disgrace."

London's mayor at the time, Boris Johnson, eventually gave in to pressure and began building lanes with curbs. Speaking to me just before he left office in mid-2016 he conceded it would have been better to not bother with the paint at all. "Looking back on it, yes," he said. "If I had my time again, and if I knew then what I know now, I would have gone straight in with a massive program of segregated Cycle Superhighways. I probably wouldn't have been reelected, unfortunately. That's one thing to consider. But that would have been the right thing to do."

The Human Measure

Another fundamental element of a useable and accessible bike network is that on smaller roads, where separation for bikes is not practical, significant speed differentials should be addressed by getting cars to slow down to about 20 mph at the absolute maximum. Such is the principle of the "cycling streets" I saw in Utrecht.

This tends to be the more difficult element to conquer.

Separated lanes tend to work pretty well, as we saw with Seville, from the moment they're built. Inspiring confidence on back roads needs subtle changes such as traffic-calming measures, speed limit enforcement, and a period of time for motorists to gradually learn that residential streets are for living on, not for speeding through.

It also requires a parallel and even more tricky official effort to make cutting through back streets less appealing by blocking off side-road shortcuts with bike-permeable dead ends or one-ways. The Dutch are extremely good at this. In many cities in the Netherlands a trip that might take ten minutes by bike could be more than twice as long by car, even if you can park at the end of it. So lots of people cycle.

Most other nations find this deliberate inconveniencing of the dominant transport culture a real sticking point. It's one of the reasons that the Seville's cycle use has yet to increase above about 6 percent of all trips. Away from the bike lanes, much of the old city remains jammed by cars, many of them parked, or crawling smoggily along at 5 mph looking for somewhere to park. Traffic reduction measures were planned, but have been put on hold by a newer, right-leaning city administration.

I can draw on an example much closer to home. The street where I live is narrow, residential, and not very long. In itself it generates very little motor traffic. But it runs between two bigger roads, and is a well-known cut-through to avoid a couple of busy junctions. And so twice a day it is plagued by rush-hour traffic, the vehicles weaving around supposedly traffic-calming narrow sections, bouncing over the speed bumps, treating the 20 mph limit as entirely hypothetical. The first few hundred meters of my son's route to school is along this road. He loves to cycle, but as it stands I will only ever let him ride along here on the sidewalk.

Hope came when the street was designated part of a so-called "quietway," a London-wide initiative to create a network of continuous routes on side roads, particularly intended for less experienced riders, or older people, or children.[13] This in part involves using already-quiet streets, but also seeking to reduce car use on other residential roads. As part of this, residents of my street were consulted on the idea of blocking off the road to all but bikes at one end, thus cutting traffic levels by about 95 percent. A majority agreed.

And then nothing. My local council retreated into paralysis, knowing they had to do this to make the quietway viable, but seemingly unable to face the wrath of the minority of car owners. A year later, at the time of this writing, we are still in limbo. I tense every time I take my son to school.

In some ways, getting out the diggers and building separated bike lanes is almost the easy bit for city authorities. For this to be more meaningful and effective requires something much more fundamental. To get a flavor of what is needed, you can look to the Dutch CROW manual, which has at its heart something beyond just a series of practical recommendations for traffic planning. In fact it's only slightly overromanticizing the 388-page guidebook to see it as being as much a work of philosophy as of road design.

It is based around a notion called "sustainable safety," which to an English ear sounds more suitably romantic in its native language: *duurzaam veilig*. By law, *duurzaam veilig* must be incorporated into the design of all Dutch roads. If I had my way it would be compulsory, daily reading for traffic engineers around the world.

It is almost absurdly simple—there are just five basic principles—and yet, if done properly, can be transformative for people who live among it. The first idea is that roads come in three types—high traffic volume through routes; local roads where a journey ends; and "distributor" roads, which link the two. Closely connected is the second key concept, that of homogeneity—big differences in size and speed should be eliminated as much as possible. So when motor vehicles travel quickly, cyclists should enjoy physical separation; without physical separation, cars must be limited to low speed. The third principle is that roads should be designed so people instantly know what sort they're traveling on.

It's on point four that *duurzaam veilig* becomes what most British and American traffic designers would probably see as worryingly hippie-ish. People are fallible, it decrees, and the road environment should be as forgiving as possible of their mistakes. This encompasses both design—curbs on bike lanes should be angled rather than straight so a cyclist accidentally veering against them is less likely to fall off—and a wider design culture that helps road users to better predict how others will behave.

Finally, the philosophy calls for people to have as much education as possible on how to remain safe, for example when to drive at certain speeds. But it emphasizes that training can only go so far, and some groups—children, for example—can't be seen as responsible for their own safety.

These five simple precepts are based around what is known as "the human measure," an acknowledgment that mistakes are made on the road and people should not pay an overheavy price for those. All this, of course, also brings innumerable benefits to pedestrians as well as cyclists.

This is the key to the role of infrastructure in reshaping towns and cities. After decades of designing urban areas for machines—cars, trucks, buses, trains, and to a much lesser extent bikes—the planners must now try to re-create them around humans.

Building for the Strong and Fearless

When the government officials do begin to focus on the humans, that's when interesting things begin to happen. In 2006, the transportation bureau in Portland, Oregon, one of the few North American cities to properly understand cycling, put out a fascinating paper that sought to create a taxonomy for the local population when it came to whether they rode, or didn't ride, a bike.[14] First among the four categories came the Strong and Fearless, those for whom even a mass of speeding traffic was no worry. Then came the Enthused and Confident, slightly less committed but still willing to ride in many conditions. Finally were the self-explanatory Interested but Concerned, followed by the No Way No How.

The first two comprised about 1 percent and 7 percent of people, respectively, the paper calculated. About a third were No Way No Hows. That left around 60 percent as Interested but Concerned: people who might be persuaded to cycle if only they felt safe. Why not, the officials concluded, start planning bike infrastructure around these people?

All this might seem a statement of the blindingly obvious. But in many countries it is a realization that has only just, if at all, begun to dawn on city planners. This is in part the legacy of decades of entrenched car-centric attitudes. But this delay in rethinking the streets can also be somewhat laid at the door of cyclists, or rather the small but dominant Strong and Fearless category, who turned their slightly niche personal preference into something of a philosophy.

This is the doctrine of vehicular cycling, hugely influential during the 1970s and 1980s. At best a sort of institutionalized coping strategy, at worst a variant of Stockholm syndrome—the psychological phenomenon that sees prisoners take the side of their captors—vehicular cycling decreed that sharing a road with the big beasts of the highway was not something to be tolerated but instead to be actively encouraged. Anyone could do it, they insisted, with just a bit of training and assertiveness.

Some of the tenets of vehicular cycling—keep your space in a lane, don't let vehicles shove you into the curb—can actually be quite useful if you're forced to ride on roads lacking bike infrastructure. But as a perceived ideal in itself, something to which to aspire, it's insanity. Experience after experience shows it limits everyday bike use to just a handful of

people, a group that includes virtually no children or older
people and remarkably few women.

The high priest of vehicular cycling is the California-
based John Forester, an exotic and occasionally belligerent
figure whose opinions colored US bike activism for decades.
In the early 1970s, he began a campaign against local laws
compelling riders to use bike lanes where they existed. This
gradually evolved into an ethos laid out in his book *Effective
Cycling*, first published in 1976 and still in print today.[15] Its
approach is summed up by this motto: "Cyclists fare best
when they act and are treated as the drivers of vehicles."

This philosophy has in recent years almost died away, although a handful of vehicular cycling advocates still hold out,
much like the tiny platoons of Japanese soldiers stranded on
Pacific islands after 1945 who refused to accept World War II
was over. The group Forester once led, the League of American
Bicyclists, abandoned his ethos about five years ago.

Anne Lusk, a Harvard University public health expert
with a long interest in cycling, recalls numerous arguments
with advocates of Forester. "My ideas would be dismissed,"
she says. "They would say: you're not a League of American
Bicyclists member; you're not a certified league instructor;
you're not an engineer; you're not a hard-core biker—you
don't know what you're talking about.

"Bless their hearts, they were male, they wanted to bike
on the roads, so they wrote the design guidelines. They
thought they could all teach their wives to bike in the road
and take a lane. And the wives said, 'I'm not going to bike in
the road.' "[16]

Their legacy, however, still lives on. The 1999 guide to building bike facilities from the American Association of State Highway and Transportation Officials, heavily influenced by Forester's ideas and only updated in 2012, focuses on "advanced or experienced riders" who are unworried about riding with motor traffic.[17]

In the UK, the semiofficial textbook for Bikeability, the UK's main national cycle training program, features plenty of perfectly sensible advice—everything from choosing and maintaining a bike to dealing with roundabouts and turns. But the publication, *Cyclecraft*, also lists among "basic cycling skills" the recommendation that riders practice increasing their cadence, the speed at which they spin the pedals, as a means of accelerating out of trouble. It advises: "A good cadence to aim for is about 80 [rpm], while a sprint speed of 32 kph (~20 mph) will enable you to tackle most traffic situations with ease."[18]

This is meant to be a "basic" bike skill: learning to change down through the gears like a pro rider and sprint away from danger. For an adult enthusiast, 20 mph is pretty quick. For a child, an old person, or a beginner, it's an impossibility.

Rachel Aldred, a cycling policy expert at London's Westminster University, says the emphasis on care and skill on the part of the cyclist rather than the wider environment is anomalous. "We wouldn't think it was acceptable if train passengers had to cross a live rail to get to a platform, and were told to 'be aware,'" she says. "We wouldn't accept a company putting up unsafe scaffolding, and the police then acknowledging this by handing out leaflets nearby saying, 'Be careful when you walk on this side of the road, you might be hit by falling planks.'"[19]

Anne Lusk, meanwhile, has her own suggestions for the few remaining and largely male proponents of vehicular cycling: "Have them bike in a skirt, have them bike with high heels, on a heavy Dutch bike with a child on the back and groceries on the front. And then have them put a purse over their shoulder and go to work. Then let's see how it works."[20]

Inspiration Out of Necessity

Even though vehicular cycling might be on its way out as an approach, no car-dominated country has, as yet, decided to acquire the Dutch or Danish design manuals and completely mimic the path taken by those countries in the 1970s and '80s. This is something much complained about by many bike campaigners, especially those in Britain, who lament that such a cycling promised land is a mere couple of hundred miles away by distance, but seemingly decades away by ambition.

And while it's largely pointless trying to cheat the basic principles of this model, as London tried and failed with its painted lanes, another key infrastructure lesson is that sometimes you have to compromise—do the best with what you've got, and accept that other elements take time. This can involve taking innovative and occasionally daring approaches.

For example, while London has lagged behind some equivalent cities in part because of its very cautious approach toward endless consultations and modeling before anything was done, New York achieved more in a similar span of time, in part by being bolder but also through improvisation.

Janette Sadik-Khan, the city's former transport commissioner under Michael Bloomberg, exemplifies this try-it-and-see approach. "There's a lot you can do with paint, and planters and stones from old bridge projects," she told me. "We closed Broadway from Times Square in a few months using only the materials we had in the transportation department's arsenal. You can change a street on a trial basis using materials that are easily adjusted or can be removed if it doesn't work out. It's available and it can be done."

Perhaps Sadik-Khan's most celebrated single change to the city's streetscape came through enforced improvisation. Just before her department was due to turn a large part of Times Square into a pedestrianized zone, a planned consignment of fixed benches and chairs failed to arrive on time. Her response was to send staff to a local hardware store to buy hundreds of folding beach chairs.

This, she recalls, ended up becoming the story rather than a route closed off to motor vehicles. "The inspiration came out of necessity," Sadik-Khan says. "Putting out those eleven-dollar beach chairs on Times Square was an interesting moment. People came out, and all people talked about was those chairs—the color, the design. Not that we'd closed Times Square to cars. It was the same experience in so many of our projects: when you adapt the street, people adopt it. It's almost like it's always been there. You go to some of these plazas now and people have forgotten the way it used to be."[21]

However valuable it can be to innovate and imagine, the converse to this infrastructure lesson is that ideas must be fundamentally rooted within what makes cycling useful and enjoyable. This is, apparently, an easy lesson for some people to miss, especially if they are architects convinced that a grand, shiny project can overcome decades of prior experience with bikes.

In late 2015, a funding drive was launched to raise the first tranche in a planned £600 million in private funding aimed to "revolutionize" cycling in London. This might sound exciting. There was just one problem: it was a very, very silly idea.

Devised by an architect and an artist, the Thames Deckway was a proposed 7.5-mile bike lane built on floating pontoons along the river Thames. Computer-generated marketing images showed smiling cyclists pedaling along a bright blue, space-age-looking structure. It was, of course, powered by solar panels. The riders looked calm, they were speeding to the other end of the city, they were safe from speeding motor traffic—this was the future!

Critics soon pointed out the flaws, not least the proposed £1.50 per trip toll needed to recoup the vast investment, likely to put off many people. The designers were also a bit vague about how they would create useable ramp access to and from a structure floating on a river with a six-meter or so height difference between peak and low tide. I asked them for an interview to explain this, and they declined to expand on their plans, which is rarely a reassuring sign.

Worst of all, the designers had seemingly forgotten why people choose bikes—it's convenient and flexible. You can choose to ride directly from point to point, or else decide to meander and stop off at shops or cafés. Neither of these options is particularly assisted by having to find a steeply ramped access point, cycle along a far-from-straight river, up another ramp, and then to your destination. The Deckway idea also forgot that another key point of cyclists is to humanize a city. They're not an inconvenience to be put to one side so the real business of moving cars and trucks around can carry on as normal.

Such red herrings, pointless and unnecessary reinventions of bike infrastructure, are increasingly common, and London seems to suffer more than its fair share. In 2014, Norman Foster, the celebrated British architect, unveiled an ambitious and deeply useless scheme called SkyCycle, 150 miles of elevated bikeways built above London's suburban rail network. It shared very similar problems to the Deckway, not least getting cyclists so high into the air without vast ramps and enormous cost.

Yet another plan decided the best place for cycle routes in London was actually below the streets, using obsolete tunnels in the Underground transit system. Amazingly, this scheme, the London Underline, won a design award.[22]

This is not to say that fast, direct bike routes are not part of the mix. Both the Dutch and Danes have in recent years begun to build special lanes intended to expand the potential range of bike commuting, especially given the increased popularity of the e-bike. Morten Kabell, Copenhagen's mayor for infrastructure, is cooperating with surrounding municipalities to create what he terms "supercycle lanes," trying to encourage people to consider a commute of up to seven or eight miles each way.

But such routes only work as part of a wider whole. A British former transport minister, Steve Norris, once very wisely described the curse of his department as "grand project-itis," a compulsion to seek expensive, shiny, overdesigned solutions to issues that could be tackled by something far more simple. The Deckway, SkyCycle, and the Underline are prime examples of how even cycling can fall prey to this. Getting more people on bikes, as we've seen above, is a fairly simple if often mundane business of introducing many dozens of incremental changes over the years. No wonder architects aren't often drawn to it.

And what of the three schemes? SkyCycle and the Underline remain nothing more than a few computer-generated images on websites. As for the Deckway, its initial crowdfunding drive flopped calamitously and was abandoned. The project remains just two people's grand, hubristic plan, and long may it remain so.

Understanding the Golf Effect

As well as getting many more people to ride, and helping to bring the urban environment back to a human scale, good bike infrastructure also has another, very significant role: it makes cycling much more safe. Curiously, a UK review from 2015 found very little in the way of rigorous academic research to prove this case. This is possibly because there seems little point, as the evidence from cities that have built bike lanes seems so compelling.

One of the most celebrated examples is New York. Data from the city's department of transport shows that from 2000 to 2014, as cycling levels grew almost 450 percent, the number of cyclist deaths stayed fairly stable, between about fifteen and twenty, while the number of severe injuries fell from 440 to 341.[23]

The department has translated this into what it calls a "risk indicator" for cyclists. Between 2000 and 2014, this reduced by 82 percent. An official graph shows the falling risk indicator and the rising number of cyclists, plotted as separate lines over the same fourteen-year period. Together they make a near-perfect X, as good a shorthand as any for the safety impact of new bike lanes.

The statistics in London are very similar. From 2000 to 2014, as cyclist numbers across London rose by 225 percent, and by much more than that within the center, the number of riders killed or seriously injured per year stayed level.[24] In contrast, across the UK as a whole, as the numbers on bikes stagnated, cycling casualties rose.[25]

Some of this can be explained by bike infrastructure that removes cyclists from potential interaction and conflict with heavy and rapid motor traffic. However, this does not explain everything, not least in London, which had almost no properly separated lanes before about 2014. There is, however, another knock-on positive effect.

This is the idea of safety in numbers for cyclists, first described in 2003 by US transport expert Peter Jacobsen, whose research concluded that when you have additional cyclists on the roads their individual risk of injury reduces, with the same effect seen for pedestrians. Jacobsen said this could be down to drivers becoming more aware of vulnerable road users when there are more of them. Good bike infrastructure makes cycling safer and more attractive, thus attracting more riders, in turn making cycling even safer. It is a virtuous circle.[26]

Some later studies have challenged elements of Jacobsen's ideas,[27] and safety in numbers remains a slightly contentious theory. But whatever causes it, there does seem to be a notable reduction in cyclist casualties when a town or city builds a coherent road network for them.

And what of the most thorough approach of all? Does the Dutch system bring safer cycling? The pretty unequivocal answer is yes. A good comparison is the UK, as the countries have broadly similar safety records when it comes to motor vehicles.

There are all sorts of ways to measure cycle safety, but one of the best is deaths per million hours spent on a bike, a formulation that takes into account not just that Dutch people ride a lot more than Britons, but that they often do so at more leisurely speeds. A 2012 study by Dr. Jenny Mindell, an epidemiologist at University College London, found the death rate for English cyclists over three years of data was 0.42 per million hours ridden, as against 0.11 for their Dutch peers, making the Netherlands nearly four times as safe. As the paper notes, this isn't strictly comparing like with like. England has many more male cyclists than female ones, and men tend to get hurt more often on bikes, irrespective of the road environment. Mindell thus reduced the infrastructure-based safety differential to 3.4.[28]

But there are other considerations to take into account, not least a phenomenon known—mainly to actuaries and insurers—as the "golf effect." This notes that while in some places, for example Florida, the number of people who drop dead playing golf is relatively high, this does not make golf in itself a hazardous game. It simply means that a disproportionate number of fairly old people, some with preexisting medical conditions, tend to play golf, and will therefore die while doing so.

For golf in Florida, see cycling in the Netherlands. So many people in their seventies or even eighties still ride bikes there that, inevitably, a certain number will keel over for the final time while on a bike and be chalked down as cycling casualties, even if being on a bike did not directly cause their demise. Saskia Kluit from the Fietsersbond points out that in the Netherlands, if someone dies within thirty days of their having been involved in a traffic crash, the crash is registered as the cause of death. This increases the official casualty rate even more.

Her organization looked in detail into more than seventy crashes involving elderly cyclists. "What we found out was that a large proportion of them broke their hip getting on or off a bicycle," she says. "Because there's a bicycle and a person the police will register it as a traffic accident. But it's just somebody getting on a bicycle. They might not even have left their front porch."

There was a spike in such incidents several years ago as many older Dutch cyclists tried out e-bikes for the first time and struggled to cope with the balance of the heavier machines, especially initial models, which often had the motor in one of the wheels. According to Kluit, studies have shown the e-bikes themselves don't tend to be ridden any more quickly than normal machines, and are no more of a risk when in motion. "But what we do see is that the bikes are heavier and people tend to topple over more than they would on a normal bike," she says. "So getting on and off the bike is now a higher-risk moment."

All this must be placed in context, she stresses: "What you have to bear in mind is that in the Netherlands about five million to seven million people a day step on a bicycle. We have about five hundred deaths a year in traffic, and about two hundred are cyclists."[29]

Dr. Rachel Aldred from Westminster University has taken this effect into account to recalculate Dr. Jenny Mindell's figures about the relative safety of cycling in the UK and Netherlands. Her conclusion? If Britain had had Dutch-style cycling infrastructure during 2012, rather than 118 cyclists dying, the true figure might have been nearer thirty-five. That's more than eighty lives saved, every year, or a death rate less than a third of what it was.[30]

Given all this, why are more cities and nations not building the sort of bike networks shown to get many more people cycling and then keep them safe? The answer, as ever, is a toxic mixture of vested interests, inertia, and a lack of political vision, which we turn to next.

CHAPTER 6

Die-Ins and Political Bravery—How Mass Cycling Happens

An unsuspecting local walking near the Saint Law-
rence River in central Montreal that day in 1975 would have
been forgiven for being a bit puzzled. Next to the water was a
group of protesters with their bikes. Standing on a rock above
them, and the focus for a gaggle of press photographers, was
a man dressed as Moses—complete with robe, headdress,
stick-on beard, and tablet of commandments. In his other
hand was a wooden staff, which he was waving vigorously,
ordering the waters to part so his people could cross.

This wasn't some esoteric piece of street theater. It was a
demonstration in favor of cycling infrastructure in the Canadian city, carried out by a then–newly formed group whose

innovative tactics exemplify many of the elements needed to successfully persuade a city to build for bikes: people power, imagination, and an awful lot of persistence.

The man in the Moses costume was Robert Silverman, aka Bicycle Bob, one of the cofounders of La Monde à Bicyclette, a loose and occasionally chaotic collective of alternative types, left wingers, and general misfits who nonetheless played a pivotal role in turning Montreal into one of North America's most cycle-friendly cities. "We went down to the riverside, me and another guy, me with a Moses costume rented from a store, with the tablets," recalls Silverman, now in his eighties. "We pretended we were running away from the Egyptians."

The stunt was to highlight the fact that decades of car-dominated city planning had left Montreal's cyclists with no way to cross the river, as they were barred from all the bridges. Earlier protests had included trying to load bikes into canoes, and halting the traffic in the middle of one existing bridge with an impromptu game of volleyball. "We called ourselves the Poetic Velorutionary Tendency," recalls Silverman. "That implied theater, and making it fun. And so we started doing theatrics."

"Most people probably thought we were crazy, but the journalists loved our events, as they were so theatrical," adds Jacques Desjardins, the only French Canadian among the group's founders. "We were on the front pages every Monday."

All this gradually bore fruit. A cycle bridge was built. City authorities also allowed bikes to be carried on the city's subway after La Monde à Bicyclette very publicly carried increasingly outlandish objects onto trains, including ladders and cardboard-cutout elephants. The group staged "die-ins," as had the equivalent Dutch protesters a few years earlier, though of course Silverman and his allies were even more dramatic, slathering themselves in ketchup to mimic blood.

While many cities experienced bike activism in the 1970s, in Montreal the protesters never gave up. The first bike lanes were eventually built in 1985, and the city now has nearly 400 miles of them, about 150 miles of which are separated from motor traffic, as well as about five thousand public-hire bikes.

While overall cycle use remains relatively low by Dutch or Danish standards, with about 10 percent of central commutes made by bike, as a transport culture it is very noticeable and has helped Montreal be included in many of the league tables of the world's most livable cities. The maverick campaigners' role in all this is acknowledged—the main bike route through the center of Montreal is named after Claire Morissette, Silverman's coleader in La Monde à Bicyclette, who died in 2007.

Desjardins says he is proud of their achievements: "All of this was the result of a citizen's movement, and not because of the authorities. We forced them to take decisions, year after year." He adds: "I think we were in many ways probably twenty years ahead of our time. What you call new urbanism—it was talked about in most places in the 1990s, but we were talking about it in the 1970s. Our first congress was about changing the city. We looked much further than the bicycle. The bicycle was a tool to change the city."

For all the romantic triumph of La Monde à Bicyclette, it should never be forgotten that the theatrics were just one part of the story. For example, while the stunts on the subway helped shape the political climate, it was a parallel challenge in the courts that prompted the eventual policy change. Getting the cycle bridge, meanwhile, also involved some more traditional lobbying of politicians for funding.

In time, this more traditional approach began to dominate. La Monde à Bicyclette, always split between Silverman's allies and a smaller cohort of Trotskyists and Maoists ("They said nothing could be done until the workers take power," Silverman recalls) soon began to fracture. Its dominant role was taken by another group, Vélo Québec, a separate and considerably more sober campaign organization that started out as a bike-based travel agency.

If La Monde à Bicyclette created the climate for Montreal's bike lanes, Vélo Québec sealed the deal. In 1985, the year the first infrastructure arrived, Vélo Québec launched the Tour de L'Île, a mass bike ride around the city. The first of these, held in autumn, was quite poorly attended, recalls Suzanne Lareau, Vélo Québec's chief executive. But the next year's one, moved to June, saw fifteen thousand cyclists. "After that the politicians realized there was a phenomenon there," Lareau says. "Then we had more and more people."

She explains: "We always had two goals with the Tour de L'Île. Firstly, it was to encourage people to use bikes and promote cycling. But the second goal was a political message.

When you have ten thousand or fifteen thousand or twenty thousand or forty thousand cyclists on the streets, politicians can't say: 'Nobody cycles here.' "

After thirty years of the Tour de L'Île, which is now the centerpiece of a weekend of bike events, Montreal's politicians ignore cyclists at their peril. The city's current mayor, Denis Coderre, is by no means a die-hard cyclist, and in fact spent much of 2015 very publicly trying to lose some weight, in part so he would be able to ride in the Tour de L'Île. "Cycling is part of our lives," Coderre told me, leaning on his bike at a rest stop midway through the event, which he did manage to finish. "People enjoy it. The city belongs to everybody, and the bottom line is to always protect the most vulnerable."[1]

Paper in a Drawer

Such talk of protest and theater can sound enticingly romantic. And it was certainly the case that in many places during the 1970s and '80s, when a move toward more bike-friendly towns and cities happened, it was mainly a bottom-up, demonstration-led process. As we saw earlier, a big impetus in the Netherlands came with the Stop de Kindermoord mass movement for child-friendly streets. In Copenhagen, up to 150,000 people massed outside the city hall in the 1970s "demanding to get their city back," as the city's mayor for roads, Morten Kabell, puts it.

These days it seems to be different. Protests can still play a role—riders in London have staged a series of high-profile "die-in" demonstrations over recent years, which have helped focus minds at city hall. But if you look at recent examples of change, the slightly sad truth is that now, whether or not your city gets bike lanes often comes down to individual politicians, and sometimes just luck.

Seville is a case in point for both. We saw in the previous chapter how the construction of protected cycle routes transformed the southern Spanish city. The story behind how this took place is simultaneously heartwarming and also a bit depressing, given how easily it could have not happened.

It all began in 2003, when the fringe United Left political alliance won sufficient city council seats to jointly govern with the Socialists. The city's traffic was in chaos at the time—because of the local habit of the afternoon siesta, it has four daily rush hours rather than two—and the United Left, traditionally supportive of cycling, managed to get a deal to build the bike lanes onto a coalition agreement. But even then it could easily have come to nothing.

By good fortune, Seville's head of urban planning was José Garcia Cebrián, a keen cyclist who, like the United Left, had been awaiting such an opportunity. Even then, he cheerfully admits, the main reason the bike lane plan succeeded was because almost no one believed it would ever happen and so very few people bothered to try and stop it.

"In Spain there's been a lot of planning about cycling, but then the plans get put into a drawer," Cebrián says. "There's a Spanish saying for documents like that, ser papel mojado, or 'wet paper'—something which is no use. That's what everyone thought the bike lane plans were. So there was no opposition during the planning process, as everyone thought the same thing would happen. The opposition only started when the infrastructure was being built, and by then there was no way back."[2]

Among the opponents were some of Cebrián's own council colleagues, mainly the car-dominated transport department. When the diggers first went out to begin work on the bike lanes, some officials were so outraged they tried to get the construction crews to halt. But it was too late.

Cebrián and the designers of the system even tried to build it in a way that would make the changes harder to reverse. Much of the space used for the bike lanes was taken from bus or parking lanes, but this was raised up to sidewalk level, so a future city government would have a more difficult job altering the layout again.

As perilous as open political opposition might be for bike infrastructure, almost as bad is lukewarm support, which evaporates the moment a noisy pressure group begins to object. Especially in the modern era of social media a relatively few number of people can create considerable volume, which in turn can spook leaders into inaction or endless delay. This phenomenon is, sadly, all too common.

The new mayor of London, Sadiq Khan, was elected in 2016 amid a string of promises to press ahead with another series of separated bike lanes, including one heading north from the city center, into some wealthy inner suburbs. There had been much consultation about this scheme, with a large majority of respondents being in favor. But within weeks of taking office, Khan announced the plan had been stopped for a review.

His decision followed a tumult of protest from a fairly limited but very well-connected group of objectors. Among the most vocal was Tom Conti, the respected British stage and film actor. In 2015, Conti issued a dire warning about what would happen to his neighborhood, the expensive North London suburb of Hampstead, if part of one road was given over to a bike lane. "The whole area will be destroyed," he boomed, predicting a "solid queue" of cars all the way to Hatfield, almost twenty miles to the north. "This is the beginning of some kind of Soviet idea to ban all vehicular traffic from London."[3]

Astonishingly, Conti's intervention was not the most absurdly overdramatic. That honor went to Nigel Lawson, a prominent former government minister, who issued a wider view on the bike lane program. "What is happening now has done more damage, and is doing more damage, to London than almost anything since the Blitz," he said.[4]

Andrew Gilligan, London's then-commissioner for cycling, treated the comments with remarkable calmness. Responding to Lawson's claims he pointed out the roadwork to build the bike lanes had caused some minor temporary traffic disruption. In contrast, the Blitz, Germany's World War II bombing raids, killed more than twenty thousand Londoners and destroyed or damaged a million buildings. As such, Gilligan argued, the two were not strictly comparable.[5]

Slogging in the Trenches

There are a few ways to overcome such skepticism. One solution, the most straightforward if arguably hardest to achieve, is to have a political patron with a big electoral mandate who firmly and publicly supports measures to achieve more cycling.

Andrew Gilligan's then-boss was the London mayor, Boris Johnson, who by the time Gilligan began introducing separated bike lanes had twice been convincingly elected by the city's voters and, unlike his successor, was very committed to cycling measures. Given such backing, Gilligan told me, he was able to treat the relatively small groups of objectors with due proportion.

"You've got to accept that any serious and meaningful cycling scheme will nearly always have clear majority support, but it will never have unanimous support," he says. "There are always going to be people who are infuriated by it. You've got to listen to reasonable objections, you've got to compromise, you've got to consult, but in the end you've got to realize there's going to be a group of people for whom no length of consultation, no amount of compromise, will ever suffice. The only thing they want is for the consultation to go on until all eternity and for the scheme to then be scrapped. In the end you've got to put your foot down."

Gilligan has a message for advocates who want to see more cycling provision: try to be as active as the objectors, especially when it comes to lobbying local politicians. "They tend to hear from the NIMBYs [Not in My Backyard], and they think the NIMBYs represent local opinion," Gilligan says. "They nearly always don't. I tell cycle campaigners: stop moaning on social media, just go and see your councilors and demand local cycling improvements."

Gilligan, a journalist with no prior city planning experience, spent the first period of his time in the job viewed with almost equal suspicion by engineers in his own administration and by London's cycling lobby groups. "At the beginning I was under attack from both sides," Gilligan says. "There was resistance from some people in Transport for London, and I was attacked by cyclists for not turning London into Amsterdam by Thursday teatime. But it was worth it in the end."[6]

A few years beforehand in New York City, Janette Sadik-Khan had faced a similar wave of opposition to a more ambitious program for bike infrastructure and new car-free areas. When Sadik-Khan (no relation to the new London mayor) became the city's transport commissioner in 2007, her hugely powerful overlord and protector was Michael Bloomberg, then the twice-elected mayor who was about to rewrite the voting laws to permit him to win a third term.

Even so, Sadik-Khan arguably faced more personal criticism even than Gilligan. She was routinely called "brusque" or "uncompromising"—even "shrill"—epithets that, oddly, often seem to be more aimed at the relatively rare women in positions of power than their male peers.

"It's fair to say that I grew a second skin over the course of six and a half years," she told me. "There's eight-point-four million people in New York and I sometimes felt there were eight-point-four million traffic engineers. All one hundred eighty acres of streets that we gave back to people on foot and people on bikes and transit was a hard-fought battle. I get it—transportation is local. People are passionate about their street, and when you talk about new ways to get around which aren't about driving, a lot of people really erupt."

Sadik-Khan agrees that having the political heft of someone like Bloomberg to take into battle was a huge help: "There's no question having a strong leader does help in establishing that vision, and supporting change when the status quo blowback begins."[7]

Nonetheless, she still faced many of the same problems later experienced by Andrew Gilligan in London. Neighborhood community boards issued streams of micro-objections, sometimes based around the loss of a few or single parking spaces. Some shop owners objected. Rival politicians latched on to the furor to demand "more consultation," even when much had been done, and had favored the scheme in question. All the while the rhetoric was fanned by an occasionally hysterical media.

Perhaps the apex of this battle was the tumult over a bike lane to be installed alongside Prospect Park in Brooklyn. Lawsuits were filed, demonstrations held, and antibike opposition groups formed with slightly sinister names like Seniors for Safety and Neighbors for Better Bike Lanes. Even after the lane was built and proved vastly successful, some court cases continued for years. It was, one local paper wrote with only slight exaggeration, "the most controversial slab of cement outside the Gaza Strip."[8]

To fight such brutal, street-by-street public relations battles, even powerful mayors and their staff need allies. At one point, Andrew Gilligan was worried that a public consultation on the bike route opposed by Tom Conti might be overcome by the energetic efforts of opponents. He appealed to those who wanted the route to take part in the survey, and it was overwhelmingly approved.

In New York, Sadik-Khan was lucky to have the assistance of groups like Transportation Alternatives, a forty-year-old campaign organization with vast experience of "slogging in the trenches" over bike infrastructure, according to its executive director, Paul Steely White. When Sadik-Khan and Bloomberg started to build bike lanes, the group sprang into action, he recalls: "We pride ourselves as smart advocates. On Eighth Avenue we literally went door to door, talking to shopkeepers and business owners, and tried to explain to them why it made sense and why they should support a bike lane. Eventually we got enough onside."[9]

Jon Orcutt, policy director of New York's transport department at the time, said the sheer vehemence of the opposition paradoxically helped prove its undoing, as it forced the city to show how much support there was for the changes. "One of the things about the backlash is it got people who measure what New Yorkers think interested in the issue of bike lanes," he says. "Your typical survey of New Yorkers is things like how the police commissioner is doing on crime. All of a sudden they're interviewing thousands of people, asking, 'Would the city be a better place with more bike lanes?' And the answer was two-thirds in favor, despite all the negative press we were getting. The backlash sowed the seeds of its own destruction."[10]

The City's Ready, Just Use Your Bike

One of the more unusual occasional jobs in local government involves dressing up in a full-length fluffy duck costume and riding a bike between preschools in Odense before handing out stickers and hugs to the children. It all sounds like innocent fun, but the duck in question, Cycling Anton, has a serious municipal purpose: making sure Odense keeps its much-cherished title of Denmark's most bike-friendly city.

Cycling Anton, who has been in service for a couple of decades, represents yet another element of efforts to get people cycling: what do you do to improve things when the lanes are already there?

In Odense, much of this involves securing the future of the city's bike culture by inducting young children into it as early as possible. As well as a hug and a sticker from a cuddly duck, initiatives include getting children as young as two traveling to kindergarten on balance bikes, offering training to nursery staff, and improving nearby cycling routes.

More widely, the city undertook what became known as

the "20/20/20" scheme—a program to boost cycling that brought a 20 percent rise in cyclist numbers, and a 20 percent reduction in bike-related crashes, and all for a cost of just 20 million krone, or about $3 million. Along with improved bike paths and parking, the city carried out projects like installing municipal bike pumps, and giving citizens the chance to try out cargo bikes. The public health savings alone were calculated at almost $5 million, with the average person in the city forecast to live five months longer thanks to the plan.[11]

About half the money went on infrastructure and the rest on promotional campaigns, explains Troels Andersen, in charge of cycling projects for the city. "It was saying, well, the city's ready, you just have to use your bike a bit more often," he says. "There's a lot of things to be done, and it doesn't always have to cost a lot. It's about getting in contact with people who want to do it because it's attractive."

Unlike places like London or New York, or even Copenhagen, Odense is not so densely built up, and many people live in a house with a garage, which requires a more interventionist approach to cycling. "We don't have the same traffic congestion, or the same parking fees," Andersen says. "Here, people cycle because it's attractive, so we need to sell the message. We are also a sales department, you could say. In Copenhagen they just build infrastructure and they get a lot of cyclists. In our way we do better. We don't have the benefits of congestion. People do it here for free. When people are cycling here they do it for the fun and pleasure, and for health."

While such efforts are, of course, built on the foundations of several decades of consistent pro-bike policies, Andersen argues that Odense is a useful template for other similar-sized cities elsewhere. "We're very average," he says. "There's hundreds of cities like this around Europe. So it's more interesting—you could have hundreds of cities like Odense, all over."[12]

In the United States, a broad parallel to Odense would be Portland, Oregon. While about three times bigger, with more than six hundred thousand residents, Portland remains relatively compact and began planning for bikes even earlier than the Danes, with its first cycle action plan passed in 1973.[13] Yet while Portland sees an impressive-by-US-standards 7 percent of all trips made by bike,[14] this is against the 24 percent figure in Odense.[15]

Jonathan Maus runs the Bike Portland website, which has in recent years become critical of what he sees as an almost complacent attitude toward cycling among city authorities. "We had a huge head start," he says. "And this is Portland, a place which has always seen pioneers and innovative thinkers, and people going against the grain. But being bike-oriented, our whole approach has been a trickle—it's been incremental, it's been small steps." Other places have moved more quickly, he says, and Portland risks being left behind.

One example Maus uses is the sedate arrival of the city's municipal bike-hire system, which has taken eight or nine years of discussions. "We wanted to be first," Maus laments.

"Now we're the sixty-fifth major city with a bike share." Agitating as he does in a small and traditionally consensual city has not always been easy, he says: "I tell you, to do this in this town is sort of heretical. I've got a lot of people upset. I've been doing this for over ten years and when I first started doing this I was best friends with everyone in city government. Not anymore."[16]

They Saw the Bicycle as the Problem

It's worth stressing that the narrative described above, of politicians and advocates moving incrementally toward more cycling, does not hold true everywhere. In China, that process has famously run in reverse. Beijing now has a little over 10 percent of commuters who brave the city's smog and increasingly feral and ferocious motor traffic to travel by bike. But thirty years ago, before China began its breakneck program of industrialization, this figure was 62 percent.[17]

China has faced some dreadful consequences with the rapid ascent of the car, not least choking pollution and anything up to two hundred thousand road crash deaths a year.[18] It's a sobering thought to consider that its leaders chose the path very deliberately, one element of a policy to create an ever-greater number of middle-class consumers.

Dan Burden, one of America's longest-standing advocates for cycling who began campaigning in the mid-1970s, recalls being accidentally at the center of this destructive policy shift. In 1994, he was among a seven-strong United Nations team invited to Beijing by the Chinese government for a seminar on bicycle traffic. Burden assumed they were there to advise officials how to best keep bikes safe on roads that were even then seeing ever more cars and trucks. He was very wrong.

"We didn't know in advance what they wanted us to do, other than help them with bicycle safety," Burden says. "So we thought: this is good. Here's a country with so many people riding bikes. But once we were at the conference it became very obvious to us that the Chinese officials wanted us to solve the bicycle problem, but they saw the bicycle as the problem. They said it was holding back the free flow of traffic. We were saying, 'No, there's just not enough room for your cars, you want more people riding bikes.'"

Eventually there was something of an impasse, Burden recalls: "I don't think we ever convinced them. But we never changed our tune. We said: you can't even project how bad your environment's going to be if you don't include the bike. The bike is actually what is going to keep your air pure, keep your traffic moving, get people places where they want to, lighten your infrastructure costs and everything. But the government officials who were there had already been given different directions—to go to a car-based society. We delivered the best we could but we simply weren't being heard."[19]

If the officials had listened to Burden, they could have saved the country a lot of current problems. Some places in China are, however, gradually returning to more bike use. Hangzhou, a prosperous city just south of Shanghai in the east of the country, has relatively high levels of bike use, in part because it never removed the bulk of its network of wide bike lanes. It has installed new bike-only traffic lights, as well as the world's largest cycle-share system, with more than sixty thousand bikes distributed around the city.

Any progress in China is, ultimately, up to those in power, given the lack of official tolerance for political lobbying. But consider the plight also of those permitted to agitate but simply face insurmountable odds.

Jack Yabut is president of the Firefly Brigade, a bicycle group with both the most evocative of names and the most difficult of tasks. Set up in 1999, the organization is based in Manila, the capital of the Philippines—a city whose traffic congestion is, according to several surveys, quantifiably the worst in the world.

The statistics are sobering. With a population of more than twelve million people, rising to fifteen million during work hours,[20] Manila has far too many vehicles for its limited road network—about four hundred vehicles per kilometer— and not much in the way of nonbus public transport.[21] As such, astonishingly long commutes are the norm.

Yabut says his nine-mile route to work would take up to two and a half hours each way by car. On a bike it's little more than forty-five minutes, even with the careful approach necessary in a city with many hazards for the cyclist: "It's dangerous for two reasons," Yabut says. "The first danger is the air quality, which is bad. We always try to encourage people to take it easy, don't exert too much effort, not more than if you were walking, so you don't get that much exposure. The other threat is the vehicular traffic. Not only is it dense here, the sheer numbers, the daredevil characteristics of Manila drivers are of circus proportions."

Yabut is still, he argues with some satisfaction, one of the very few Manila residents to get some fun from their commute. "I'm used to it," he explains with a laugh. "I've been commuting by bicycle since the late eighties. And it's enjoyable, really. I take different routes, I'm not rushing, I just relax, take an hour. But if I'm in a rush I'll take the main highway, and be with all the other traffic. The good thing about it is that all the cars are in gridlock. The bicycle is the only thing moving."

Despite his years of campaigning, Yabut estimates there are still no more than fifteen thousand cyclists riding around the city, more than a few years ago but nothing compared to the three million–plus motor vehicles. "We've grown since 1999, but if you put that alongside the extent of the problem, we're still a way off," he says. "At least now there are some people in government who are listening to us, and entertaining the idea of integrating the bicycle in transportation development, but we're still at a very early stage."[22]

They Knew Exactly What to Do with Their Streets

All these varying political narratives can seem complicated, and it can sometimes be hard to draw any common lessons. But there are a few. From my limited experience, based on writing about cycling and dealing with the questions, objections, and insults that follow, whether on social media or in person, it does seem bike advocates can achieve a lot, if they choose.

To begin with, as Andrew Gilligan notes, they must be wary of mistaking Twitter or Facebook for the real world, and instead should engage on a neighborhood level with the people who actually make the decisions that affect them. This might seem a bit prosaic and painstaking when the alternative is to post sweeping social media manifestos on how you'd transform your city, but there's no denying it gets more done.

In the previous chapter, I mentioned the paralysis of my local council in South London over making the difficult decisions to curb car use on the road where I live, which is supposed to be designated as a so-called "quietway," suitable for everyday cycling.

When it became clear the council was sitting on the issue in the hope it would be forgotten, I went with a neighbor to see our local councilor. We sat down with her over a coffee and explained, as patiently and politely as we could, that keeping the street as it was would mean the "quietway" designation was utterly meaningless. Beforehand, I borrowed a small video camera, attached it the back of my bike, and rode up and down my street at a leisurely pace one morning rush hour to capture the current experience for cyclists on film.

The councilor, to her credit, looked a bit shocked when we showed her the footage of impatient drivers tailgating me, or squeezing past at speed. Our case was possibly helped because the most aggressive van, shown driving about an inch from my back wheel, carried the very obvious logo of the council itself.

Will this achieve anything? At the time of this writing I genuinely don't know if it will. The scheme is still mired in seemingly endless consultation. But we might have helped change a mind. And that's the important bit.

More widely, a good message for activists is to frame the arguments beyond just bike lanes, or reducing car use. With road space in cities necessarily finite and the era of knocking down buildings to provide more room for cars now well and truly over, there's no escaping from the fact that new solutions are needed to congestion and pollution, as well as the other problems that come with urban living.

Chris Boardman—the British Olympian and Tour de France cyclist–turned-campaigner for cycling—says he has a standard rejoinder to those who tell him they oppose the construction of new bike infrastructure. "If anybody wants to object I totally respect that," Boardman says. "But I would say: if you're going to object you must give me a viable alternative. I think that's a fair way to have any kind of debate or discussion."[23]

In the Netherlands, the head of the country's cycling organization, the Fietsersbond, says she likes to put the question in a similarly broad way. "I don't usually ask people about traffic or bike lanes," says Saskia Kluit. "I ask them: what sort of environment do you want? Because there's not a single person who will raise his hand and say, 'I want to live next to a busy car road.'

"So you will have everybody saying, 'Oh, it would be nice

if we had more trees, it would be nice if we had less traffic, it would be nice if we had more space.' And when they've spoken you can say, 'If you want to achieve that, then we need to take car spaces, have a separate bicycle track, and then we can have more trees to make it nice.' And then everybody's happy."[24]

For politicians the message is clear: Be bold. Build the lanes. Block off the backstreet car cut-throughs. Don't take half-measures, as they will end up pleasing nobody. And remember, if you show sufficient vision and push through some decent cycling infrastructure, then it will be used, and by more people than you can imagine. The same is true for all changes to give streets back to people, whether on foot or on two wheels.

Janette Sadik-Khan recalls the moment when she first realized that the political risks of making New York less car-dominated were going to pay off. It was August 2008, and the city was experimenting with one of her earliest projects, the so-called Summer Streets program, where almost seven miles of central roads were closed off to cars for three Saturday mornings in a row, so people could cycle, run, meet, or do whatever they chose. The idea was not new—Bogotá introduced its equivalent, La Ciclovía, in the 1970s—but it was entirely untested in New York.

"I remember, hours and hours before it opened, being out on the streets with my team and looking around, thinking, 'What if no one shows up? What if this is a disaster?' " says

Sadik-Khan. "I remember being truly relieved when I saw people walking and biking, and kids out there playing. We had three hundred thousand people coming to play, and cha-cha, and take basketball lessons. It turned out New Yorkers knew exactly what to do with their streets."[25]

Such boldness is all too rare when it comes to rebuilding streets such that more than a minority who drive cars get proper use of them. There is a good argument that it should no longer be even seen as bold or daring, just obvious and necessary.

Paul Steely White believes it is high time cycling infra-structure becomes viewed "not as an optional amenity that is open to local veto, but really as a necessary public safety improvement that we now make in these modern times."

He argues persuasively: "It would be akin in the time of cholera saying, 'We've got this engineering approach that involves separating our water from our sewage, and it involves digging up the street—what do you think about this? Are you okay with this?'

"There's a way to design streets now that kill many fewer people and are much fairer, more equitable, and more efficient, and we're just going to do it, dammit."[26]

CHAPTER 7

If Bike Helmets Are the Answer, You're Asking the Wrong Question

The bill introduced to Wyoming's legislature by a Republican member, David Northrup, could be described as extremely thorough in its approach to cyclists' safety. Anyone riding a bike in the state should have a flashing light at the rear, and carry some photo ID, it said. Oh yes, and be wearing high-visibility clothing in fluorescent orange, pink, or green—visible from the front and back, covering at least two hundred square inches in area.

Some local cycling advocates, however, were a bit less certain. Brian Schilling, who manages a network of cycleways in the Jackson Hole area of the state, said he was largely in favor of cyclists having rear lights. "But the orange vest—I think that's a little onerous," he mused. "My five-year-old kid, I don't think her entire surface area is two hundred inches."[1]

Some months later a representative in another state legislature, Jay Houghton, had his own flash of inspiration. All cyclists wanting to use minor roads in Missouri, his bill decreed, must fly a flag "no less than fifteen feet above the roadway." Again, bike advocates had their worries, not least that a fifteen-foot flagpole would snag on most bridges, even electricity cables. One St. Louis bike shop bolted a sufficient-length pole and flag to a child's bicycle and tweeted a photo of the result—an ungainly, top-heavy creation that looked like it would knock over the bike in the slightest breeze. Houghton was not deterred. "My constituents, who drive these roads daily, feel this is a good idea," he told a local cycling advocacy group. "I believe in freedom, and this bill in no way restricts your freedom to ride on the roads."[2]

You could just chuckle and say such proposals, neither of which became law, are little more than the strange goings-on and attention-seeking antics common to many smaller legislatures—in this instance from politicians who simply don't understand a type of transport that very few of their constituents actually use. Sadly, that's not all there is to it. Representatives Northrup and Houghton can just as credibly be seen as slight outliers of a very much more mainstream opinion. This contends that cyclists are uniquely responsible for their own safety, and that the use of sufficient high-visibility clothing, along with a cycle helmet, is by far the best and most important way to overcome the disadvantages of unsafe road infrastructure and poor driving. This philosophy, which can be fairly described as blaming the victim, often extends also to pedestrians and to children. It's so common that surprisingly few people even challenge it.

Take an event a year or so ago at Signhills Academy, a school in Cleethorpes, a small town on the northeast coast of England, where a class of students ages ten and eleven were visited by construction multinational Balfour Beatty. A company representative handed out high-visibility vests, with the exciting news that the child who wore theirs most often in the coming months would win a bicycle. "The vests are really important as children can do strange things on the road and many walk to school," head teacher Ken Thompson told the local paper. Meanwhile Dave Poucher, the Balfour Beatty senior traffic engineer handing out the vests, said: "We do it to get the message across that safety is everybody's business, from birth until death."[3]

From birth until death. This is astonishing, appalling stuff. Of course, making sure children know roads are dangerous places, and that too many car drivers drive overly fast and don't always concentrate, is a sad and basic necessity of modern life. With my own son, I try to avoid scaring him about life in general. Motor traffic is the exception. Here, it's almost hard to overstate the risks.

But why simply accept this? Those "strange things" children do presumably include being impulsive and distracted. In other words, being children. And yet it's they who are told they must adapt to a hazardous traffic system. A ninety-pound child is seen as facing an almost equal burden of responsibility for traffic safety as does an adult driving a one-ton vehicle. Ken Thompson and Balfour Beatty might have spent their time and effort more productively in agitating for slower and rigidly enforced urban speed limits for cars.

The common rejoinder to all this is for people to say: of course drivers must be careful, but surely everyone else must do what they can. In many ways it's a fair argument, but it ignores one vital point: it is only roads where we see this supposedly shared culpability.

Airline passengers are not told to wear high-visibility jackets and look carefully for taxiing planes when walking across the airport tarmac to catch a flight. The same Cleethorpes parents who waved their children off to school in high-visibility vests would presumably be aghast if the head teacher suggested the youngsters be drilled from infancy to carefully taste their school lunches and decide if they were okay to eat, as the cooks in the canteen would do their best to not use rotten meat but sometimes just lost concentration and got it wrong.

Let's clarify one thing immediately: I don't object to helmets, or to high-visibility clothing. I wear a helmet most of the time when I'm on a bike. So do most people I know in London. But when it comes to genuine efforts to make cycling safer, they're a red herring, an irrelevance, a peripheral issue that has somehow come to dominate the argument. You don't make cycling safe by obliging every rider to dress up as if for urban warfare or to work a shift at a nuclear power station. You do it by creating a road system that insulates them from fast-moving road traffic.

Chris Boardman expressed an eloquent opinion on this when an innocuous appearance on a television news program to discuss bike infrastructure became dominated by angry viewer reactions to him being filmed cycling down a street bare-headed. "I understand exactly why people feel so passionately about helmets or high-vis," Boardman wrote. "I understand why people wish to use them. But these actions seek to deal with an effect. I want to focus the debate on the cause, and campaign for things that will really make cycling safe. That is why I won't promote high-vis and helmets—I won't let the debate be drawn onto a topic that isn't even in the top ten things that will really keep people who want to cycle safe."[4]

Boardman is not alone in finding that helmet use provokes strong and strange reactions. Nick Hussey, the founder of a British cycle clothing company, Vulpine, became so perturbed by the vicious social media reaction when his firm's website featured models on bikes without helmets, he wrote a response for my newspaper's cycling blog. It began with the parallel of him hypothetically marching into a bar and snatching a third or fourth beer from a random drinker's lips, yelling, "Stop drinking or you will die!"

"That's more or less what the infamous helmet debate has become," Hussey lamented. "Shouty strangers shouting at other shouty strangers for choices that don't affect the first shouty stranger's life. It's a bit weird, definitely a waste of energy, and not a fun place for cyclists to share space in."[5]

I'm with him on that. So, to reiterate: I have no issue with anyone wearing or not wearing a cycle helmet, or indeed high-visibility clothing. I do, however, have very serious worries about efforts to make use of high-vis clothes or helmets compulsory, or even to overly encourage them as a supposed safety panacea. They're not. As Chris Boardman also noted, in the Netherlands, perhaps the least perilous country for cyclists in the world, helmets and high-vis are almost unknown.

Asking the Wrong Sort of Doctor

Dr. John Black is a very eminent doctor of emergency medicine. Formerly a consultant at one of the UK's foremost hospitals, the John Radcliffe in Oxford, he has managed helicopter acute medical teams and advised the government on emergency care. He has seen, firsthand, the terrible life consequences that can follow from a head injury on a bike, which evidence shows can often be worsened if the rider is not wearing a helmet. He's therefore precisely the wrong person you should ask about whether helmet use should be compulsory.

Why? It's because Black necessarily sees only one rare and extreme side of what is a complex and nuanced issue.

Black believes helmets should be obligatory by law. He was among a series of doctors who wrote to the British Medical Council, which represents the profession, requesting that it formally call for mandatory helmet use. It subsequently did, a decision that remains controversial and much debated.

Black told me he sees his views as "simple common sense," believing legislation is the best way to increase helmet use. "If someone's unprotected head strikes a solid surface such as the roadside or the pavement, even if it's a ground-level fall, patients can sustain devastating head and brain injuries," he explains. "We know that the wearing of cycling helmets can reduce the risk of that by up to two-thirds."

Black says he has treated young people who suffered such injuries that left them unable to live independently. "I just don't think we can afford to plan for particularly young people of working age potentially being incapacitated and needing lifelong care, with all the devastating consequences that has, not just for them but for their families," he says. "I don't think we can afford to be complacent about this issue."

All this makes perfect sense, does it not? Let's hear, however, from another doctor. Dr. Harry Rutter is a public health expert who specializes in physical activity. He cowrote a chapter on cycle safety for the influential handbook *City Cycling.* "Helmets do not create safety," he said. "Only a safe environment, free from the dangers created by motorized traffic and poorly designed roads, can do that." He is skeptical about an excessive focus on helmets as a safety measure. "Most of the risk of severe injury while cycling is not intrinsic to the activity—motorists impose it on cyclists," he argued. "Cycling is a benign activity that often takes place in dangerous environments. Of the three main elements determining serious cycling injuries—the road design and conditions, the motorist, and the cyclist—the cyclist is the most studied."[6]

If I want an expert on one patient's head trauma, then Black is the doctor I'd choose. But Rutter is an epidemiologist, and so looks at issues on a population-wide level. And the problem with the helmet debate is that too few people do this.

But let's begin with something hopefully straightforward and more individual: if you happened to fall off your bike and strike your head, I'm pretty certain a well-fitted and properly fastened helmet would offer some injury protection. Not everyone agrees. If you read an online debate about bike helmets—and I really don't recommend it—even this can be a surprisingly contentious position to take, with endless talk about whether risks from extra rotational neck injuries caused by a helmet might negate the lessening of head trauma. But the evidence is pretty strongly in favor of a net reduction in injury.

It's worth stressing that even this has limitations. For example, the EU bike helmet standard promises protection in a drop test up to speeds of 5.52 meters per second, or just over 12 mph.[7] That will probably help in many of the sort of low-height secondary impacts described by John Black, but nothing much more serious.

Nonetheless, most studies indicate a benefit. A major 2001 review of the research concluded that helmets reduce the risk of head injury by 60 percent.[8] A 2011 examination of this piece by Rune Elvik, the Norwegian academic and road safety expert we met in chapter 2, said the overall protection could be slightly reduced given what seems to be an increase in the likelihood of a neck injury if you wear a helmet. But it is still very much there.[9]

Now, however, things begin to get more complicated. Whatever the benefits in each individual case, Elvik notes, a population-wide increase in helmet use, for example after legislation, is not generally matched by similar reductions in overall head injury rates. How can this be? Surely a nation of cyclists entirely kitted out with helmets will be notably less prone to injury than those riding bare-headed? Well, yes and no. Again, with helmets things are never as straightforward as they appear.

Close Passes and Unconscious Assumptions

Robert Chirinko is a man with a minor obsession for spotting how people's behavior changes according to their perception of risk. Thus, he notes, while a small car actually might be less safe if someone is actually in a crash, recognition of this fact makes a person more likely to drive carefully, and they may well end up safer overall. The advent of mobile phones has left Chirinko wondering if some people now take more risks walking alone at night, as being on the phone can give an illusion of connectedness and thus protection.

He also has thoughts on the plague of serious concussions affecting American football. "Is the solution more padded helmets and other protections? Offsetting behavior suggests that more protections lead to a greater feeling of safety, and hence an increase in the severity of tackles, blocks, and other confrontations," he says. "It follows that the solution may well be less protection. If US footballers feel less safe, they will surely temper their performance on the field accordingly, with desirable health outcomes for all participants."[10]

Chirinko is an economist at the University of Illinois, not a doctor or road safety expert. But his ideas about offsetting behavior, his profession's term for what psychologists call "risk compensation," is a fascinating element to the discussion over bike helmets. Most crucially, it can work two ways: it seems the perception of reduced risk from helmet use can both prompt riders to be more reckless with their own safety and nudge drivers into being less careful toward cyclists.

The idea of risk compensation canceling out safety improvements is not new. In *Death on the Streets*, a 1992 British traffic safety polemic, author and transport expert Robert Davis notes that the invention of the methane-detecting Davy safety lamp for miners in 1815 actually saw more deaths initially, as it prompted mine owners to send workers to shafts seen previously as unworkable for safety reasons.[11]

Davis also argues that a 1983 law to oblige British drivers and front-seat passengers to wear seat belts might have improved their safety, but at first did little for that of others. A government-commissioned report two years after the law came into effect, by two professors of statistics, found that crashes involving cars had seen a 40 percent rise in cyclist deaths and 14 percent more pedestrian fatalities.[12] Truck drivers remained exempt from the seat-belt law; the number of vulnerable road users they were killing had not risen.

One of the most famous experiments connected to risk perception and cycle helmets was carried out by Dr. Ian Walker, a psychologist at the University of Bath, and a man who has researched attitudes and reactions to cyclists with more thoroughness than most. In 2006, he attached a computer and an electronic distance gauge to his bike and recorded data from 2,500 drivers who overtook him on the roads. Half the time he wore a bike helmet and half the time he was bare-headed. The results showed motorists tended to pass him more closely when he had the helmet on, coming an average of 8.5 centimeters nearer.[13]

Walker said at the time he believed this was likely to be connected to cycling being relatively rare in the UK, and drivers thus forming preconceived ideas about cyclists based on what they wore. "This may lead drivers to believe cyclists with helmets are more serious, experienced, and predictable than those without," he wrote.[14]

Such half-conscious assumptions can involve more than just helmets, Walker found. In a parallel experiment he also spent some time riding about wearing a long brunette wig, to see whether drivers gave female cyclists more room than men—perhaps because they also assume women are less experienced. They did, it emerged, even when the "woman" was six feet tall and, for the drivers who happened to look in their rearview mirror, surprisingly hairy.

The converse to all this is yet another study carried out by Walker, this time in 2016, which appeared to show a parallel effect to this: that helmet use could potentially make cyclists act in a more reckless fashion.[15] His experiment saw participants of various ages and both genders asked to play a computer game in which they pressed a button to inflate a balloon on the screen. Each inflation earned them more hypothetical money, but also increased the random chance of the balloon bursting, which would wipe out the winnings. At any point players could stop and "bank" what they'd earned from each individual balloon.

Those taking part were fitted with eye-tracking sensors and told this was the purpose of the experiment. However, the sensors were not plugged in—the real test was that half the participants had the eye tracker fitted to a baseball cap, the other half to a bike helmet. Over dozens of games, those wearing the helmets consistently took greater risks on average when inflating the screen balloons.

Walker said this was the first time apparent risk compensation had been identified even when there was no direct link between the improved safety and what the person was actually doing. "The helmet could make zero difference to the outcome, but people wearing one seemed to take more risks in what was essentially a gambling task," he wrote. "The practical implication of our findings might be to suggest more extreme unintended consequences of safety equipment in hazardous situations than has previously been thought."[16]

All these variables come into play when considering helmet use. Yes, a helmet might make you safer if you get knocked off. However, it might also, even marginally, increase the chance that this happens in the first place. And it's when a government decides it needs to pass a law making helmet-wearing compulsory that we start to see even more unintended consequences.

"Australians Love Rules and Regulations"

City-wide bike-share programs have become increasingly common in recent years, spreading to hundreds of places around the world. These have almost invariably proved hugely popular. Not, however, in Australia. Melbourne and Brisbane both launched systems in 2010. Both are widely viewed as flops. While bikes in the equivalent London and New York systems get ridden anything from about three to six times a day each, their unloved peers in Melbourne, generally seen as Australia's most bike-friendly city, are lucky to be used once. A study found the system in Brisbane was the least popular in the world, with each bike ridden just two in every five days on average.[17] In part this is down to flaws in the networks—both are relatively small and spread out. But there's another factor at play: helmets.

If you ride a share bike in London or New York or Paris or Hangzhou, you can bring a helmet if you want, or otherwise just leap on and pedal away. Do the latter in Melbourne or Brisbane and you risk being stopped and fined by police, because of compulsory helmet-use laws in force since the early 1990s. Both programs have tried to get around this by leaving complimentary helmets on the bikes—Melbourne leaves one thousand new ones a month—or selling cheap helmets at nearby shops. But for many people it's simply too much bother.

This is one of the many accidental effects of helmet compulsion. Even in a youthful, vibrant, and otherwise innovative city like Melbourne, a bike-share program is a nonstarter. A small if significant opportunity for creating a human-friendly city is lost.

Clover Moore, the lord mayor of Sydney for more than a decade, says she would also love to create a bike-share system there but feels unable to, given the long-standing helmet compulsion law. This comes from the government of the surrounding state, New South Wales, over which she has no control. "I'd like to do it, but with the helmet law it's not viable," Moore says. "Australia has a reputation for being a free and easy nation. And the very opposite is true. Australians love rules and regulations, or at least our governments do."[18]

At some point during such a discussion, a proponent of helmet compulsion will usually say something along the lines of: "Forget all this talk about freedom or inconvenience. If a bike helmet law saves just one life, then it will be worth it, surely?" This is emotive stuff. But the accidental effects of bike helmet laws can go much further than just undermining bike-share systems. Strange as it may initially sound, there is evidence that they can end up causing more deaths than they save.

This is down to the apparent deterrent effect helmet laws

have on cycling. Some studies have indicated that they put off enough people from riding bikes in the first place that the resulting negative effect on public health more than cancels out any benefits from fewer head injuries. As with everything connected to this subject, it's worth noting that it's all bitterly disputed by opposing sides. But the evidence seems solid.

One study carried out for New South Wales transport authorities in 1993, a year after mandatory helmet use for adults in the state was extended to children, was mainly intended to check whether the new law was increasing helmet uptake. This it had—but the researchers also found a 30 percent reduction in the number of children riding to school.[19] Similar data showed even bigger reductions in bike use in other parts of Australia when helmet laws came in. In New Zealand, where helmet compulsion was introduced in 1994, the number of overall bike trips fell 51 percent between 1989–90 and 2003–6, according to one research paper.[20]

The reasons are mixed. It can be in part because some people simply don't want to bother with a helmet, a factor arguably less important now than twenty-plus years ago, when bike helmets were more expensive and not nearly as comfortable. More pressing, however, appears to be the fact that obligatory helmet use reinforces the notion that cycling isn't an everyday way to get about, but a specialist pursuit needing safety equipment, which makes it less appealing.

Professor Chris Rissel, a public health expert at the University of Sydney, carried out a 2011 study that asked people in the Australian city about the effect of the helmet-use law. It found almost a quarter that said they would cycle more if they did not have to always think about a helmet, with the greatest increase in bike use among younger or occasional cyclists. A repeal of the law would, Rissel said, have a significant positive impact on improved public health.[21]

Another Australian academic once tried to quantify this effect. Piet de Jong, a professor of actuarial science at Macquarie University, crunched figures for the estimated reduction in bike use if helmets are made compulsory against any fall in head injuries. "For most countries, under assumptions favorable to the helmet legislation case, the unintended health costs cancel out the direct health benefit," he found. For the US, de Jong calculated that an overall net cost to public health of a helmet law would be $4.8 billion a year.[22]

Critics have questioned some of de Jong's calculations. However, there are other potential health drawbacks to helmet compulsion. For a start, if a law does mean fewer cyclists, you have the possibility of a reverse "safety in numbers" effect, the phenomenon we saw in chapter 5—fewer riders on the road could place those remaining at more individual risk.

All this illustrates the problems of asking someone like John Black for their opinion on helmets. His specialization means he comes across the minority of people who have, in his words, "had a bad day." It's his colleagues in general medicine, however, who deal with many hundreds of times more patients whose lives have been similarly blighted by diabetes, heart disease, high blood pressure, strokes—all conditions strongly associated with a lack of exercise. It can be a difficult connection to make, but it's an important one.

Evidence, Not Anecdote

Callous as it might sound, along with a doctor of emergency medicine, the very last person you want to ask about cycle helmets is a relative of someone who has suffered a head injury while on a bike. In 2010, the British Olympic rower James Cracknell was taking part in a charity cycling event in America when his head was struck by the wing mirror of a passing truck. He suffered a severe head injury but survived, in part because he was wearing a helmet. His wife, Beverley Turner, a TV presenter, has since become a vocal advocate for their compulsory use.

Turner's approach is highly emotive. "I don't really care about the macho twits who duck in and out of city traffic wearing headphones but no helmet, without a thought for the mothers and girlfriends who will pick up their pieces," she wrote in a newspaper column a few years later.[23]

I understand Turner feels strongly. That said, she understandably sees just one side of the issue. Turner could have written something else, just as inflammatory but at least more relevant for the bulk of people in modern Britain: "I don't really care about the lazy twits who duck in and out of fast-food restaurants eating burgers but taking no exercise, without a thought for the wives and children who will pick up their pieces of their diabetes or stroke or heart attack."

This can be a difficult argument to make. However, proponents of mandatory helmets seek to present themselves as being led by evidence, so it seems right to approach them on those terms. The only part of the UK to have introduced such a law is Jersey, one of the mainly self-governing Channel Islands in the waters between England and France. In 2014, the States of Jersey, the island's centuries-old combined legislature and executive, passed a law compelling children thirteen or under to wear a helmet, at pains of a £50 fine for their parents.

In many ways, wearing a helmet makes even more sense for children than it does adults. They have a greater likelihood to fall off bikes and, when they do, are more likely to hurt their heads, in part as young bodies are disproportionately weighted toward the skull. My son wears a helmet whenever he's cycling. That said, there is currently no evidence that Jersey's law will achieve anything at all.

The island's government commissioned the UK's respected and independent Transport Research Laboratory to evaluate the plan. Its report found that the year before the ban was imposed, 84 percent of Jersey children wore helmets anyway, and not a single under-fourteen had been seriously hurt on a bike.[24] So even if the law suddenly meant every child wore a helmet, which is unlikely, that's still a sixteen-percentage-point protection improvement for zero casualties.

At the time, I spoke to Andrew Green, the Jersey politician behind the law. He dismissed the idea that it would see a reduction in cycling, but offered only an anecdotal argument as to why: "I believe children participating in cycling will increase after the law, based on the number of phone calls I've had from parents saying, 'I want little Johnny to wear a helmet. He won't wear it because his friends won't wear one.

Therefore I won't let him have a bike.' "[25] It's an argument. But it's not evidence.

The tragic backstory to Green's interest is that his now-adult son is unable to live independently after he suffered a serious head injury on a bike when he was nine. Green himself chairs Headway, a charity that does fantastic work with people who have suffered brain injuries but has branched out, controversially, as a vocal advocate of helmet compulsion.

As with Beverley Turner, it's easy to see why Green does what he does. It can be difficult to counter his views, but equally it's important that someone does. Of its annual budget of £630 million in the year the law was passed, Jersey's government spent precisely £150,000 on "pedestrian and safety improvements."

This is a compact island with a benign climate and lots of green space. Yet 23 percent of its five-year-olds are overweight or obese, rising to 35 percent of children ages ten or eleven, higher figures than in the rest of the UK. When it comes to improving the health of children, the government might be better served doing everything it can to get them on bikes, not passing laws that overexaggerate the dangers of doing so.

While Jersey has been passing a law based, seemingly, on anecdote and personal experience, one of the most prestigious peer-reviewed scientific health publications in the world has twice published papers examining the impact of helmet compulsion. Both times it has found the case, at very best, unproven.

In 2006, the *British Medical Journal* carried an examination of the evidence by Dorothy Robinson, an Australian statistician, into what actually happened in New Zealand and Australia after helmet compulsion laws were passed. This research backed the contention that they can reduce the number of cyclists, especially children. One automated bike counter in Perth, Western Australia, saw falls of 20 percent, 24 percent, and 35 percent, respectively, in the amount of riders in the three years after the legislation. "All available [long- and short-term] data show cycling is less popular than would have been expected without helmet laws," Robinson concluded.[26]

The study also uncovered complications over figures that do seemingly show a reduction in head injuries suffered by cyclists following helmet compulsion laws, a fact much touted by advocates. For example, it found evidence that adult cyclists who opt to wear helmets tend to be more safety-conscious anyway, while helmeted children are more likely to ride in parks rather than streets. So, even as helmeted cyclists suffered fewer head injuries, they also had fewer serious nonhead injuries. As is so often the case with dubious science, correlation did not necessarily equal causation.

Finally, the study noted, helmet use laws had often come into force at the same time as other road safety measures, such as random driver alcohol breath testing in parts of Australia, which was likely to have even more impact on safety. The conclusion? The idea that bike helmet laws directly improve overall safety for cyclists doesn't appear to be backed by any evidence from countries where these laws have actually been passed.

Another *BMJ* paper looked into helmet compulsion laws in Canada, passed by various provinces from the midnineties onwards. The 2013 research found provinces that had made helmets mandatory did see a quicker reduction in cyclist head injuries than those that did not. However, the same thing had been taking place before helmet compulsion. Again, the connection could not be safely made. The researchers concluded: "We were unable to detect an independent effect of legislation."[27]

Why is the public and government narrative about helmet use in some countries so at odds with the evidence? For this we turn to yet another *BMJ* article, in this case an opinion piece written by two experts with a knack of making complex concepts easy to follow—Dr. Ben Goldacre, a doctor who has a parallel media career debunking poorly written science articles, and David Spiegelhalter, professor of the public understanding of risk at Cambridge University.

Even such a pair confessed they had reservations about tackling the subject. "We have both spent a large part of our working lives discussing statistics and risk with the general public," they wrote. "We both dread questions about bicycle helmets."

The article looked into whether helmets do protect individual users and then whether promoting or mandating them brings a wider public health benefit. It was a vexed issue, they said, and almost impossible to determine anything meaningful amid a complex scientific methodology, over which were laid various layers of politics, culture, and belief.

"Supporters of helmets often tell vivid stories about someone they knew, or heard of, who was apparently saved from severe head injury by a helmet," the article said. "For others, this is an explicitly political matter, where an emphasis on helmets reflects a seductively individualistic approach to risk management."

Their very slightly depressing conclusion? The noisy arguments will continue indefinitely, with virtually no one having their view swayed either way. "The current uncertainty about any benefit from helmet wearing or promotion is unlikely to be substantially reduced by further research," they predict. The popularity of bike helmets as a road safety measure was based less on any direct benefits, they said, but more so on people's often very skewed personal perceptions of risk.[28]

Seeing, but Choosing Not to See

While much of the cycle safety debate centers around helmets, high-visibility clothing has an equally pernicious role to play, as with the pupils of Signhills Academy. Again, the unquestioned assumption of 90 percent of the people you talk to about the subject is that wearing a tabard or waistcoat in a lurid Day-Glo color is a boring but utterly necessary part of being an urban cyclist.

The converse is that not wearing one somehow makes you partly to blame for a crash, whatever the actual cause. A friend of mine was once knocked off her bike by a car that steered toward the curb, pushing her onto a sidewalk. Visibility was perfect, she could clearly be seen, and the distracted driver completely culpable. And yet when her mother heard about the incident, she sent her daughter a high-visibility waistcoat in the mail. The mother meant well, but the implied message is poisonous.

Again, I have no issue with people using or not using high-visibility gear. But it's important to stress how irrelevant it is in the wider safety argument.

In 2013, Britain's Transport Research Laboratory looked at twelve studies on the issue going back to 1969. This centered on motorbikes, in part because there is much more research on how they can remain visible to drivers. The report found one study that seemed to show that drivers saw moving motorbikes more quickly if there was a greater color contrast between the background and the rider's clothes. Another concluded that, depending on the road and traffic, the most visible rider apparel could be a high-vis jacket, a white jacket, or even a black jacket.

"The results are interesting in that they show the previously held assertion that a bright reflective jacket will improve rider conspicuity may not always be true," the TRL investigators wrote, saying people "need to be aware of the limitations" of efforts to be seen.[29]

In other words, high-vis might well help you to be seen. But it's not the solution to everything.

The most fascinating and, in many ways, alarming study about what cyclists can realistically do to protect themselves amid poor road infrastructure also centers on highly visible clothing. Inevitably, it was conducted by the tireless and ever-imaginative Dr. Ian Walker (who is, I should stress given how often I've mentioned him, no relation).

In 2013, Walker carried out a more extensive version of his helmet study. It also measured how closely drivers passed a bike when overtaking, but this time he tried out seven different outfits. Four made him look like a cyclist of varying experience and dedication, ranging from full Lycra to more everyday clothes, as well as one involving a high-visibility jacket. Three other outfits were based around bright yellow waistcoats bearing written messages. One read NOVICE CYCLIST: PLEASE PASS SLOWLY; another said, POLITE: PLEASE SLOW DOWN—"polite" is sometimes used by UK cyclists and horseback riders in the hope drivers might mistake it for "police"—and finally one read, POLICE: CAMERA CYCLIST.

Walker gathered data for just under 5,700 overtakes and discovered something very interesting: none of the outfits made an appreciable difference to driver behavior, apart from the one saying "police." For the six others, the average passing distance was between about forty-five and forty-six inches. For "police" it went above forty-eight inches. Similarly, the proportion of drivers who went very near the bike was noticeably lower for the "police" vest. In contrast, the tabard saying "polite" saw the nearest average overtaking distance and almost twice as many potentially dangerous passes as "police."[30]

The lesson seems clear and worrying. Drivers were perfectly able to distinguish between different types of rider, and to read and absorb any message displayed. But rather than adjusting their driving to the perceived experience of the cyclist, it was only when faced with a threat to their own welfare—the sight of what seemed to be a police rider—that many allowed a cyclist more space on the road. Most alarming still, some seemed to treat the mild attempt at deception of "polite" as a reason to almost punish the cyclist.

Walker is too professional to put it in such strong terms. But he admits to worries. When he carried out the 2006 helmet experiment, he says, he did not conclude that the results meant drivers didn't care. "I felt that was a very callous interpretation, and it was more likely that they just took the helmet as an indication of experience," he says now.

The later study changed his view, Walker explains: "It really might have been something like, 'Well, he's got a helmet, it doesn't matter.'"[31]

This is yet another layer of context for the debate about helmets and high-visibility clothes. Dress up like a Day-Glo beacon, some still argue, and even if this does end up putting other people off cycling, or even bringing a net disbenefit to society, at least drivers can see you.

However, Walker's last study raises a frightening proposition, one that plenty of regular cyclists in places like the UK, the United States, and Australia would probably recognize. Far too many drivers can see you perfectly well, it seems. When they skim past you at high speed, it could just be that they don't especially care for your welfare. I certainly recognize that picture from my own experiences.

How can that be possible? What sort of rotten, skewed road culture would see drivers put a fellow human being at minor if appreciable risk, seemingly just for the sake of it? There are lots of possible answers, which we look at in the next chapter.

CHAPTER 8

The Outgroup: Why Cyclists Are Hated

Of Scorchers and Outgroups

A letter writer to the *Times* newspaper in London had very definite ideas about cyclists. "It is the practice of a number of them, spread out across the road, to rush down at headlong speed, more like a horde," they wrote. "Woe betide the luckless man or aught else coming in their way."[1] The sentiments might be very modern, but as you can possibly guess from the language this was not a recent letter. It was, in fact, published in 1892, as complaints about overfast cyclists—popularly known as "scorchers"—became increasingly common in the press.

Such was the extent of the anticyclist feeling, little more than a decade after their mode of transport was invented, that some writers felt a need to hit back. In 1896, the English popular satirical magazine *Punch* carried a mocking riposte titled "New Rules for Cyclists." Each bike rider is "presumed in all legal proceedings to be a reckless idiot, and on the wrong side of the road, unless he can bring conclusive evidence to the contrary," read one supposed diktat. Another jokingly decreed that if a cyclist saw another vehicle or a pedestrian approach on the road, they should "instantly dismount, run the machine into the nearest ditch, and kneel in a humble and supplicating attitude till said horse, cart, etc., has got at least a mile away."[2]

If the tone at all feels oddly familiar to readers in places like the UK, the United States, Australia, and New Zealand, that's because in some places the public discourse about cycling seems barely to have advanced in the last 120 or so years, except for "scorcher" being replaced by "Lycra lout," "spandex warrior," or another variant. Ride a bike in many cities, and it can feel like you're the unelected local representative of some mistrusted, barely understood cult. I occasionally experience this from work colleagues, relatives, and friends. Sometimes the questions are based around curiosity ("So, why do you all wear such funny clothes?"), or can be more openly hostile ("Why do you all run red lights?"). It's what I imagine it must be like being a Mormon or a Scientologist.

Why does it still happen? The most straightforward answer is that in places where such attitudes prevail, cyclists do tend to be a small minority, often not vastly more numerous than, say, Mormons. But there is more to it. There is strong evidence that cyclists are treated like what psychologists like to call an "outgroup."

In the simplest terms, an outgroup is the "them" in a "them and us" scenario. Human beings inevitably seek association with others, for all sorts of reasons. The unfortunate corollary of this instinct is the desire to exclude those who don't fit in. "It can be any situation in which some group or category difference comes to the fore in people's lives," says Rupert Brown, professor of social psychology at the University of Sussex. "It can work two ways—taxi drivers might think all cyclists jump lights, while cyclists in turn think taxis are badly driven. It's a relativist thing. It depends on your own vantage point."[3]

Outgroups tend to feel most beleaguered when they are numerically small, and are scapegoated or stigmatized by a significantly larger or more powerful section of society. The most traditional and pernicious variant of this is, of course, things like race, nationality, religion, or culture. But it can also be applied to incredibly heterogeneous groups with nothing more in common than, for example, that they happen to ride a bike as one of their ways of getting around.

Some academics who have studied attitudes to cycling believe it suffers in such a way. "Definitely. It's something I've talked about a lot," says Dr. Ian Walker, the British psychologist whose many studies about the way drivers treat cyclists we saw in chapter 7. "What you see in discourses about cycling is just the absolute classic nineteen sixties and nineteen seventies social psychology of prejudice," he explains. "It's exactly those things that used to be done about minority ethnic groups and so on—the overgeneralization of negative traits, underrepresentation of negative behaviors by one's own group, that kind of thing. It's just textbook prejudiced behavior. It's not so much the number of people. It's to do with power. In this case it refers to power to own the street, as it were."[4]

This modern power relationship between cyclists and society is not a straightforward interaction. In places like Britain and elsewhere, the lack of a culture of everyday cycling means a disproportionate number of people who do use bikes tend to be enthusiasts, often male, and sometimes riding relatively expensive machines. Thus, some of this mocked and despised group, in other areas of their life, might actually be relatively privileged and powerful.

In 2013, *The Economist*, the weekly bible of the management classes, ran a completely serious article calling road cycling "the new golf," identifying it as the best way for businesspeople to network with one another.[5] A couple of years earlier a leading market research firm, Mintel, published a study noting that the modern British cyclist is disproportionately likely to have an above-average household income.[6] In some ways these people are the spiritual descendants of the Victorian "scorchers," hobbyists for whom a bike is often a choice rather than necessity. There are still plenty of people who cycle only because it's convenient, or they can't afford a car. But it is not these who are stereotyped in the media as the default for every cyclist.

Rachel Aldred, the Westminster University transport expert we heard from in earlier chapters, argues that in some of the scorn for cycling comes from this characterization of it being somehow frivolous—unlike the serious, adult business of driving a car. "It's as if you're doing something you shouldn't be doing on the roads, almost like you're playing in the street and getting in the way of the traffic, like you're a child," she says. "There's also this dual way you can be stigmatized as a cyclist—it was historically seen as something for people with no choice, but now it's seen as something for people who have a choice. It's a leisure or play thing that they shouldn't be doing in this inappropriate place."[7]

Does any of this really matter? Can't cyclists, especially the middle-class, above-average-income-earning ones, just shrug it off? To an extent many do. But there is a problem: the moment anyone is obliged to ride a bike on a busy road, the power balance tilts alarmingly. Those nineteenth-century cyclists faced a relatively equal traffic environment of pedestrians and carts. Their modern successors are still just flesh, blood, and bones, but now matched against people inside speeding metal cages.

This is why the cyclist-as-outgroup idea is so harmful. The media clichés inform a wider narrative in bars, in offices, and on the Internet. This in turn infects the sentiments of politicians who, seeing cyclists as despised and mocked, are less likely to risk implementing pro-cycling initiatives. Finally, there is evidence that the way people view cycling can affect the way they actually drive. Studies have indicated that this outgroup status can prompt drivers to give people on bikes less space, or to automatically assume they are in the wrong. Very recent research even suggests, tentatively, that negative media coverage can bring an increase in anticyclist incidents on the road.

All of a sudden the subject feels a lot more serious.

They Want to Confiscate Our Road

To unpack the way cycling is too often portrayed in the media, let's look at a 2015 editorial opinion column in the *Staten Island Advance*. I've got no particular wish to target this long-running publication, which has the honor of being the only remaining daily paper specific to a borough of New York City. But it's illustrative, not so much for the opinion itself—an argument against plans to build more local bike lanes—but for the way it is expressed.

"Ardent bicyclists, we've found, have an evangelical zeal about their pursuit," the op-ed begins. "For the most passionate of them, it's not enough that they enjoy cycling; they insist that everyone must enjoy it." This "fervor," the paper says, has found "eager acolytes in government."

Consider the language. Cyclists are "they," against the paper's—and, implicitly, the readers'—"we." They are "evangelical." They don't have supporters in government, they have "acolytes."

The column condemns the city government's pro-bike policies: "So it is that bike lanes have been superimposed on street after street throughout the city, regardless of capacity or traffic conditions, as lane space for car and truck traffic is confiscated to allow the addition."[8] Again, it's the language that is telling. Road space is "confiscated," meaning it must have been owned, in this case by drivers.

The piece goes on for some time. Cycle advocates are "devotees," "true believers," "hard-core enthusiasts"; their ideas are "radical thinking." Building more bike lanes is "wishful thinking" and "fantasy." It's the sort of language you'd expect to be used for a religious cult, not a group of people who'd just kind of like it if they and their friends and family were able to cycle around a bit more easily and safely. The subtext is fairly explicit: cyclists are both an "other" and a homogenous mass to which you can ascribe all sorts of shared characteristics.

I always find this latter element particularly baffling. Strictly speaking, a cyclist is just someone who chooses a bike as one of what is probably several means of transport, or forms of leisure. It is true that some people feel a more tribal affinity with cycling. They might read bike magazines, even hang around in bike shops chatting about tires and chain lube. But even those who approach the *Staten Island Advance*'s idea of a "devotee" will probably also watch TV, or perhaps play chess. They might babysit for nephews or nieces, enjoy superhero films, go out for meals or on vacation. And yet it's only the one activity that is meant to define them.

These generalizations can creep into the utterances of people who would otherwise consider themselves impeccably liberal and inclusive. Take Linda Grant, a British writer who actually began her career as a journalist for my newspaper, *The Guardian*. Grant is learned, thoughtful, and award-winning. Along with novels, she has written a celebrated feminist history of the sexual revolution. And yet when it comes to cycling all those subtleties evaporate.

In late 2015, Grant wrote a column (again for *The Guardian*) that in part described the difficulties she faces, given her impaired eyesight, crossing London streets down which cyclists can sometimes zip at high speed. There are the beginnings of an interesting subject here. A few cyclists, as with all road users, can be reckless. While very rarely lethal, their behavior can be more intimidating than they maybe think, especially for more vulnerable pedestrians.

But Grant overlays this idea with a thick layer of hugely sweeping statements. Cyclists are, she notes, "the most morally pure of road users, the ethical standard-bearer for healthy living, a challenge to climate change." There are exaggerations: "In a normal day of pedestrian road use I can repeatedly observe cyclists running red lights, and also coming up on to pavements scattering screaming passersby." Grant stresses that not all cyclists are like this, but it's a limited concession: "The percentage of arsehole cyclists may be a minority, but it's a minority large enough to make crossing roads an exercise in guesswork."[9]

This kind of language fascinates me. I like to speculate what sort of other hugely varied group to which Grant might ascribe common, unifying characteristics and failings. Vegetarians? Painters and decorators? She could perhaps write: "The percentage of arsehole great-aunts may be a minority, but it's a minority large enough to make going to tea parties an exercise in guesswork." Of course not. If she did, the response from readers would be in part anger, but also just bafflement.

These are just two examples, and both of the milder variety. Much of the outgroup talk is more blatant. *The Daily Telegraph* newspaper in Sydney, Australia, has spent years consistently and repeatedly labeling cyclists as red-light runners and law breakers, and condemning any plans to make the roads more safe for them.

One of Britain's most respected political columnists, Matthew Parris, once wrote a column in the *Times* titled, "What's smug and deserves to be decapitated?" suggesting people should string piano wire across cycle paths. As we'll see later, a few people actually do this. And yet the suggestion—later explained by Parris as a joke—was arguably among the less offensive parts of the article, which labeled cyclists as oddly dressed, self-righteous, impractical, badly mannered, angry, self-satisfied, and "insolent jerks."[10] *The Spectator*, a venerable British current affairs magazine, once devoted its cover story to a diatribe calling cyclists oversensitive law breakers who deliberately hold up traffic while wearing "pompous little pointy plastic hats."[11]

In places where the outgrouping is most strong, such talk tends to coalesce around the modern-day folk devil known in the UK as the "MAMIL," an acronym for "middle-aged man in Lycra." This semimythical creature rides shiny and expensive road bikes, squeezing its white-collar belly into unflatteringly tight cycle clothes. Such people, the discussion goes, are not just weird-looking and antisocial, they're also smug, self-righteous, and apt to moan like sissies every time a car passes within six feet.

Time and again, otherwise sensible and clever writers lapse into stereotypes and generalizations. All cyclists jump red lights, they wear funny clothes, they don't pay for the highways. They ride in the middle of the road. They're a menace to others, and to themselves. They're them. They're not us.

There Isn't a War on the Roads

When I discuss this subject with someone, there generally comes a moment when they pause, look a bit awkward, and tell me: "Of course, these generalizations are bad. But cyclists do jump red lights a lot, don't they?" My response to this is usually on the lines of: "You live in London. There are idiots everywhere. Why do you only notice the idiot cyclists?"

I don't mean to excuse poor behavior by cyclists that, as I mentioned above, can be genuinely antisocial and intimidating. I don't like cyclists running reds or bunny-hopping onto the sidewalk to weave between pedestrians. If you're a healthy twenty- or thirtysomething trying to avoid such riders, they are an irritant. If you're old and terrified of a fall, or walking with a small child, it can be deeply unnerving.

Some riders argue that ignoring traffic lights is the safest option amid a traffic system intrinsically biased against them. Personally I disagree. I think people mainly do it because it's more convenient for them.

In fact, there is a good argument that the worst sorts of cyclists are quite likely to also be aggressive and risky when they drive a car. On a train they're probably the sort to push past you to grab a seat. When flying they probably recline their seat all the way back the moment the meals are served. They are, to borrow Linda Grant's word, arseholes. But unlike her I blame the person, not the mode of transport. These are multimodal arseholes.

The problem for cyclists is that their law-breaking is highly visible. It's easy to tut as someone blithely cycles across a junction on red, but you might not have noticed all the motor traffic doing 40 mph–plus in a 30 mph zone, let alone the drivers glancing down to look at a phone screen on their lap. This sort of behavior is normalized, even though it's statistically much, much more likely to kill or maim someone. This can sound like a plea on behalf of reckless cyclists. It's not. It's just a plea for proportion and for context.

Occasionally one of the people discussing cyclist law-breaking with me will suggest that miscreants should have their bikes immediately confiscated and melted down. Fine, I reply: just as long as the same rules apply to drivers. No scrapyard on Earth would be big enough for a single day's haul from one of the main roads of London, New York, Paris, or Sydney, let alone Beijing or New Delhi.

A slight modification on the narrative is the idea that drivers and cyclists are engaged in a somehow equal battle for space and supremacy, often described as "a war on the roads." This is silly for several reasons, not least that in many countries the majority of cyclists also drive, and so are supposedly at war with themselves. In reality, the idea is mainly used as an excuse to suggest onerous and pointless regulations for cyclists, on the supposed idea they are on a par with cars.

In 2015, the very cozy and respectable BBC radio con-
sumer program "You and Yours" discussed whether cyclists
should be obliged to take out third-party insurance, an idea
inspired by an incident where a sidewalk-riding cyclist struck
and slightly injured a young child.[12] Chris Boardman, the
Olympic cyclist who now campaigns for everyday cycling,
was a participant in the program, and very politely pointed
out how rare such events were.

Afterward, Boardman was considerably more blunt,
telling me that the whole premise for the program was absurd.
"When you put it into perspective, there are thirty-six people
in the UK killed on sidewalks by cars, buses, and lorries every
year—that's just on sidewalks—versus about one every three
years from a cyclist," he said. "It's ludicrous the program was
even on. Nobody seems to feel obliged to look at any facts."

Boardman is more scathing still about the idea of a "war"
on the UK's roads. "You've got two percent of vulnerable
road users versus ninety-eight percent in two tons of steel,"
he said. "How can you possibly have a war? I think that's
called a massacre."[13]

It's impossible to gauge how much this affects politicians, the
people with the actual power to improve life for cyclists. It's
fair to say that at either end of the political commitment scale
it probably makes little difference. Michael Bloomberg had
clearly decided by 2006 that his city needed its streets re-
shaped, and wasn't about to let a few hostile headlines in the
New York Daily News sway him. Equally, Toronto's late and

troubled former mayor Rob Ford had a seemingly more fundamental antipathy at work when he started digging up bike lanes, telling citizens that "roads are built for buses, cars, and trucks," and if a cyclist was killed "it's their own fault at the end of the day."

My own theory is that the outgroup notion comes most into play for politicians who maybe feel they should do something for cycling, but don't manage to treat the subject with sufficient seriousness. In part this is because, as a transport minister, commissioning a new rail line or airport is much more exciting than thinking about prosaic bike lanes and a few redesigned junctions. But I'm convinced that too many politicians just don't see cycling as a necessity. For them it is an add-on, a sop to the enthusiasts, something to be squeezed onto a road if there's a bit of spare space and spare cash left over from the main task of motor traffic. This, I fear, is where the outgroup notion can shape their thinking.

It might help explain why some otherwise sensible politicians, like their equivalents in the media, can start talking utter nonsense when they discuss cycling. Some of these are gaffes that, if said on a more mainstream subject, would see them ridiculed, even drummed from office.

At the time of writing, Robert Goodwill had spent several years as the British junior transport minister whose brief covers cycling, among other areas. Goodwill is a diligent politician who presents himself as the cyclists' friend. When I interviewed him soon after he got the job he pointed proudly to the folded Brompton bike in the corner of his Westminster office, on which he dashed about London. And yet, when

Goodwill was speaking to a parliamentary inquiry into cycling in May 2016 and was asked why relatively so few British women ride bikes, he gave an alarming response. There are several genuine and interconnected reasons for why this happens, almost all connected to poor bike infrastructure. Goodwill, however, breezily recollected how his wife had once told him she worried about getting "helmet hair" if she rode a bike.[14] This is the man with ultimate responsibility for cycling in the UK. We should despair.

Amazingly this wasn't even the silliest thing said by the person in Goodwill's role. His predecessor, Norman Baker—also keen and intelligent, also occasionally clueless—was once being quizzed by MPs about cycling safety, and asked what lessons the UK had to learn from the Dutch. His answer wasn't just alarming, it almost defied belief.

The statistics, Baker explained patiently, showed the Netherlands actually had a higher cycling casualty rate than the UK. "What we can learn from the Netherlands, in my view, is probably not safety issues, particularly," he said with some smugness.[15] MPs and members of the public scratched their heads. As we heard earlier, cycling in the Netherlands is generally seen as being three or four times safer than in the UK.

It transpired Baker was talking about cycling casualties per head of population, a measure which takes no account of the fact the average Dutch person cycles about ten times farther every year than their British peer. It was the sort of basic statistical error that would see a teenager mocked in a math class. Baker might as well have congratulated himself on the much lower British casualty rates connected to windmill repairs, speed skating, or tulip picking.

They're Doing It Again

It is, however, to Australia, where we must go for the arguably best example of an overtly hostile media setting the tone for politicians. How bad are things there? Bad enough for a veteran bike campaigner to write a mock letter from a future government apologizing to cyclists for treating them so dreadfully.

Written by Omar Khalifa, formerly head of Bicycle New South Wales and now leader of a new cyclists' political party, his letter from a hypothetical future state government echoed a recent apology by police to the organizers of the first gay Mardi Gras in Sydney, the New South Wales capital, in 1978. While Mardi Gras is now a much-celebrated part of the city's cultural landscape, many of the first participants were arrested and beaten up. The parallel might sound extreme, but Khalifa argues it is relevant. "They're doing it again," he says. "They're not bashing people, but they're cracking down with harshness."[16]

Khalifa was prompted to act by new laws introduced in New South Wales state in March 2016, which immediately increased fines for offenses such as not wearing a helmet or riding dangerously up to sixfold, pushing some to 425 Australian dollars (about $310 USD), and also set a date in 2017 for riders to carry obligatory photo ID.

The regime was devised by the state's roads minister,

Duncan Gay, a man who once proudly described himself as the government's "biggest bike lane skeptic," and who had previously proposed the idea that cyclists should be registered and licensed. This was dropped after civil servants pointed out it would be almost impossible to implement, would bring no real benefits, and would be likely to put a lot of people off cycling.[17]

In its place came the new fines, along with a concessionary move to oblige drivers to give cyclists at least a meter of space (around three feet) when overtaking, rising to one and a half meters (closer to five feet) if passing at more than about 40 mph.

Sensible enough stuff, surely, to encourage all groups on the road to behave better? It's not so simple. Treating cyclists as a problem to be regulated into submission simply ends up meaning fewer people ride bikes. Even before the new fines, an onerous regulatory system underpinned by compulsory helmet laws introduced in 1991 has kept cycling levels in the state pathetically low, at around 2 percent of all trips. It could be much more, especially in Sydney. The city is spread out and hilly in places, but it has obliging weather and a lot of inner suburbs in easy riding distance of the center.

I spent a gloriously happy couple of years there as a bike messenger, enduring a couple of earlier police crackdowns on cyclists. The most memorable and most ludicrous saw an unhappy contingent of officers sent out on bikes to pose as couriers, an undercover role not helped by their middle age and bulging waistlines. I once saw a member of this squad chase a colleague of mine up a hill in the city center, yelling for him to stop. The colleague, among the top ten amateur road bike racers in the state, was so unfailingly polite he would surely have stopped if only the policeman had gotten close enough to be audible.

Some elements of the city's bike culture have improved since then, mainly thanks to Clover Moore, Sydney's mayor since 2004. She is keen to see more cycling and has built some separated lanes. But her powers are limited, and Gay and his state government seem determined to block her at every turn. They are egged on by a media obsessed with the supposed need to tackle dangerous, law-breaking riders, with phrases like "speed demons" and "reckless cyclists" common. The city's *Daily Telegraph* newspaper, in particular, seems obsessed with the subject.

Moore describes the overall effect as "toxic." She told me: "I've had daily attacks in that newspaper over the years. But it's not just the *Daily Telegraph*. We committed to a two-hundred-kilometer cycle lane network in Sydney, and some people considered this an absolute revolution. I had television cameramen based outside my house to film me. I was so outrageously attacked from the start."[18]

Traffic laws and the policing of them are a matter for the state, and some Sydney cycling advocates say the new fines and the zealous and varied way in which they are enforced are making cyclists feel less welcome than ever. One of the $425 fines is for dangerous riding, something local police appear to interpret as they choose. One early receiver was stationary at a red light but track standing, where you keep the bike balanced but motionless while on the pedals. Other riders have been stopped by officers and warned they could be fined just for cycling on busy roads.

Khalifa believes Gay's overall tone makes cycling even more marginalized, and thus more risky. "He's resonated with those people in the community who see cyclists in front of them as being an obstacle," Khalifa says. "It becomes a venting of frustration."

Gay himself doesn't tend to talk much in public about cycling, perhaps because when he does he occasionally says some very odd things. During a 2014 TV interview he was asked whether it worried him that helmet compulsion could put some people off cycling. Not a bit of it, Gay responded. If people who don't like helmets don't cycle at all, that would definitely keep them safe, he said, adding with the grin of a man who believes he's clinched an argument: "I've saved their life."[19]

At the time, Gay was pondering the cycle registration scheme, something he justified on the supposed basis of cyclists needing to be protected from their own risky behavior. "We need to change the actions and the habits," Gay said. "If we have a system of rules that people know can be enforced, they will think about what they do on a particular day."

I asked Gay's department several times if I could interview him but was rebuffed. I was instead granted a long chat with Bernard Carlon, head of road safety in the state. As an official rather than a politician, it is Carlon's job to come up with evidence to support the minister's decisions, and I'm far from convinced he's done so. I asked Carlon several times why, if helmet use was the key, countries like the Netherlands had far better safety rates for cycling and almost no helmets. He replied that Australia's road environment and "culture of cycling" are very different.

What Carlon sees as the main argument for tougher enforcement measures is the fact that data from health authorities shows that 30 percent of cyclist injuries in New South Wales don't involve another vehicle, but instead a rider falling after hitting a curb or pole. The inference is that cyclists are riding in a risky and reckless manner, and must be somehow reined in through huge fines and compulsory ID checks. If you were Dutch or Danish, you might instead begin by looking at the infrastructure on which all these cyclists keep crashing. But then if you were Dutch or Danish, you wouldn't have a media telling you every day that cyclists are a feral subsection who need taming.

Omar Khalifa is among those convinced that the way cyclists are written and talked about has a direct influence on the laws they face. "As an advocate I've too often heard, 'It's you guys, you cyclists,' " he says. "Imagine turning it around and saying, 'You motorists,' because you saw someone go through a red light. That would be inconceivable. But when you're a minority group you tend to take all the bigotry, and tend to be classified as a group, and it's therefore justified doing anything you want to all of them."

Sabotage

It is not only Australia. Ian Walker is among those who believe the UK also sees a connection between the way cyclists are discussed and the occasionally reckless way people act toward them. "I'd be very surprised if that's not happening," he says. "It is acceptable to sit in a pub and say things like, 'Bloody cyclists, we should run them off the road,' or to write things that are, literally, calling for murder. You can't do that with other groups. Firstly, the fact it's acceptable to get away with that, and people aren't castigated for saying and writing these things, tells you a lot about where we stand. And it would be incredibly surprising if the fact that people are saying and writing these things doesn't then shape perception of how normal an act it is."[20]

One of the most comprehensive studies about the social status of cyclists was carried out in 2002 by Britain's respected Transport Research Laboratory.[21] The researchers spoke in depth to dozens of drivers of varying types during focus groups. Those interviewed often displayed stereotypical outgroup opinions of cyclists, who were seen as low status (this was shortly before the MAMIL phenomenon emerged) and also unpredictable.

Many drivers were puzzled why cyclists "didn't pay for the roads." Commonly used words included "irresponsible," "despised," "erratic," and "arrogant." This wasn't constant—drivers who also cycled and, to a lesser extent, women were inclined to be more sympathetic. But such negative opinion seemed prevalent.

There was more to it. As part of the study, the drivers were shown videos of various interactions between vehicles and cyclists on the road, including cars pulling out in front of bikes or turning across them. The research found that, even when a driver was clearly to blame, the focus groups tended to criticize the cyclist, seeing fault as innate to their status.

"The respondents' comments indicated that they thought the cyclist's actions were inherent and dispositional behaviors," the researchers wrote. "In contrast, the motorists' misdemeanors were excused or justified in terms of the situational influences."

Crucially, while the drivers were at pains to insist that they themselves were always patient and careful with cyclists, they predicted that other drivers would be notably less so. This is what's known as "norm positioning," a psychology term that explains people's tendency to describe the habitual behavior of others with some accuracy while unconsciously boosting their self-esteem by saying, with less honesty, that they would, of course, behave far better themselves.

The report's conclusions are phrased in slightly blank academic language, but the implications are nonetheless chilling: "An important point following from this analysis is that it seems unlikely that drivers' own behavior actually is as cautious as they claimed it to be, since the norm positioning effect entails adoption of a somewhat artificial stance. In other words, the true 'social norm' for behavior around cyclists is probably less tolerant and less cautious."

So, bias against cyclists means drivers who hold such views are inclined to give bikes less time, space, and patience on the roads than they should to properly protect such a desperately unprotected and vulnerable road user. But why? The authors argue that as well as seeing cyclists as an outgroup, drivers feel a "strong obligation" to other members of their motor-powered ingroup to not delay them, even if that means passing a cyclist recklessly. All this is pretty depressing, but of little surprise for someone who has cycled regularly in the UK, or somewhere else with a similar bike culture.

Sometimes the hatred of cyclists as a group can be expressed much more explicitly. In June 2015, Alec James was taking part in an organized ninety-mile mass bike event on closed roads through countryside in South Wales. But his day ended early. "I was about thirty miles in, on a fast downhill stretch, and I saw one rider on my left go down," James says. "I moved to avoid him and started to slow. Then my front tire blew out and I went over. I rolled with the bike for a good few yards, bashed my head, breaking the helmet. I was doing about 30 mph. I got deep lacerations on my leg. I couldn't walk properly for a week."[22] When he got to his feet, to find a pedal-shaped chunk taken out of his thigh, James saw the crash had been caused by dozens of tacks deliberately spread across the road.

A couple of weeks earlier, several riders taking part in a race on the back roads of Surrey, to the south of London, suffered punctures after tacks were scattered. That no one was hurt was mainly down to luck, says Adrian Webb, chairman of the cycling club involved: "You can guess how dangerous it can be if you have an eighty-man peloton and someone punctures unexpectedly. These guys have got slick tires pumped up very strongly for a race—there's every chance a tire can explode. If a rider comes off, there could be a mass pileup."[23] Such tactics seem peculiarly common in the UK, which has also seen a spate in recent years of wire strung along off-road bike tracks, something also seen on a few US trails.

Not everyone agrees that such actions are connected to negative coverage of cyclists. "There are about 250,000 assaults on the streets a year," Chris Boardman says of the UK. "If we're going to accuse other people of taking things out of context, we need to not do that. There are always going to be idiots and people who are evil or just plain stupid." Others disagree. Mark Strong, a cycling advocate in the English seaside city of Brighton, connects incidents there of wire strung across bike paths to the introduction of new cycle lanes by a Green-led council. "There is an element of legitimization toward dislike of cyclists from the attitudes of the press and politicians," he says. "It's almost an official endorsement to be anticyclist. And for everyone who thinks it's now okay to shout at a cyclist, at the tip of the bell curve there will be somebody who think it's okay to stretch wires across bike paths."

One recent Australian academic study indicates that Strong might have a point. Research by the Accident Research Centre at Melbourne's Monash University saw cyclists in Australian Capital Territory, a state with high bike use and also a significant number of road collisions involving cyclists, fitted with helmet-mounted video cameras and GPS data loggers.[24]

About 450 hours of footage was recorded during more than five thousand miles of commuting trips. While none of the participants was knocked off, the study recorded ninety-one "potential conflict events," most commonly drivers turning across cyclists or car doors being opened in their path. As an aside, more than 90 percent of the incidents were found to be the driver's fault, though you could argue this was skewed by the expectation that cyclists fitted with cameras for an experiment are less likely to be reckless.

Most relevant here is the interview stage of the study, where the cyclists described their experiences on the roads. A number of them told the academics that they noticed a definite increase in harassment from drivers following a high-profile and much-reported fuss when the retired Australian cricketer Shane Warne called for cyclists to be licensed after getting embroiled in an argument with one when driving his car.

One participant, a woman in her forties, said: "When we had the Shane Warne incident in Melbourne, for about two or three weeks I copped so much abuse on the road, but after that it's toned down. So I think that [driver abuse] peaks with those incidents."

A lot of the participants recalled a similar upsurge in aggression before the study, in 2009, after a popular Australian satire show, *Good News Week*, ran a skit in which two comedians discussed their frustrations with cyclists, and mimed opening a car door onto them. One cyclist in his fifties said he was harassed three times in a single commute a couple of days after the show was broadcast.

This is not forensic proof. This was a qualitative study involving thirty-six cyclists, and any connection was reported by them. But it's potentially alarming stuff.

"What Is Something Annoying a Cyclist Might Do?"

One of the many oddities of the language and tone used against cyclists is how few other such disparate groups endure similar treatment, other than over issues such as religion or culture. Jokes about mothers-in-law and female drivers are largely of the past. Even Britain's ferocious tabloid press has stopped referring to people with mental illness as "crazy" or "bonkers" following pressure from charities.

One British cycle campaigner, Mark Treasure, makes a fascinating if slightly contentious comparison between the tone taken toward cyclists and that taken in the 1970s and '80s against people who followed football in England. While English football is now a glossy, corporate, multibillion-pound, TV-funded operation, in that earlier era fans tended to be working-class and, due to occasional violence at games, dismissed en masse as hooligans. The culmination of this process was the Hillsborough disaster, one of the worst civilian tragedies and longest-running injustices in recent British history. It took place in April 1989, when ninety-six Liverpool fans were crushed to death after supporters were herded into a too-small, fenced area of a crumbling stadium. While this was primarily down to police blunders, officers made up stories about drunk, rampaging supporters. Despite a lack of any evidence, this became the official narrative and was not formally corrected until 2016.

Treasure notes that British cyclists are also labeled as law breakers, unworthy of proper treatment. "These attitudes and opinions are then used to legitimize claims that cyclists don't deserve any kind of 'special treatment'—i.e. cycling infrastructure—that would reduce risk of serious injury or death," he writes. "The comfort and conditions of cyclists is regarded as moot."[25]

Let's end with a very modern equivalent of our opening 1892 complaint about reckless scorchers. Rather than a letter to the *Times*, the medium was a TV quiz show, *Family Feud*, known to British audiences as *Family Fortunes*. For those who haven't seen it, the program pitches two teams of families against each other to guess the most common answer to largely inconsequential questions put in advance to a panel of the public. This is the Australian edition, hosted by Grant Denyer, a toothsome and chipper figure who bounds around the set, beaming at everyone. Here, he grins more broadly still as a question comes up: "What is something annoying that a cyclist might do?"[26]

A wholesome-looking young woman from one of the competing families pushes the buzzer to give what proves the most-given answer: "Ride in your car lane." Amid the appreciative applause there's no explanation of what a "car lane" might be, and how it differs to an ordinary lane on the road.

Next, the opposing family takes over the guessing. "Cutting you off," correctly guesses one young man. A relative tries her luck. "I'm a bit of a fashion person—they wear Lycra . . ." she begins, bringing a snort of laughter from Denyer. "Do you find that a little, um, offensive to the eyeball?" he asks, to understanding giggles from the audience.

The remaining answers as to why cyclists might be annoying are, in ascending order of popularity, "ringing the bell," "riding slowly," "pulling out in front," "running red lights," and "everything." Each is treated as gently amusing, the unspoken subtext being that all the contestants drive cars, while cyclists are a slightly exotic and exasperating alien group.

Such limp humor might seem a long way from wires across paths, or even a road environment that only the most confident and assertive of riders feel they are able to brave. But the connection is there. Every complicit grin from Grant Denyer, each assertion from Duncan Gay that cyclists must be regulated into safety, op-eds in the *Staten Island Advance* describing roads "confiscated" from cars, Linda Grant's decision to write a column about morally pure arseholes—it all adds up. Every one of these, I am convinced, places me, my loved ones, and anyone else on a bike, marginally yet incrementally in more danger every time we get onto a saddle. And that can't be right.

CHAPTER 9

Two-Wheeled Technology

Strava is a hugely popular app that uses GPS signals from phones or other devices, allowing people to map and upload their bike rides, and then compare their endeavors to those of other users. The San Francisco–based offices of Strava are much as you might imagine for the city's booming tech industry. In one section of the airy, concrete-floored space, engineers type code, full-ear headphones drowning out the surrounding chatter. A mezzanine floor formerly earmarked for extra desks is instead used for yoga classes. Everyone drinks endless cans of the flavored fizzy water stacked inside huge fridges in the kitchen.

In a quiet corner of the building is a tier of raised wooden benches built into a sort of small semicircular amphitheater. This is where, every few months, the company holds something called the Strava Jam—at which any employee can throw out ideas, however unlikely or untested. It was that meeting which saw the accidental beginnings of one of the more fruitful recent collaborations for high technology and everyday cycling.

Strava holds huge amounts of data, on who cycles where and when, from around the world. But at first, the company had no idea how to make this useful. Then engineers at a Strava Jam came up with the idea of building heat maps— overlaying the bike data onto digital street plans to visualize the numbers riding. "At the time it was really cool, but we didn't really know what to do with it," admits Mark Shaw, the company's chief technical officer. "So we just released it to the public on our website."[1]

Most of those who saw and played around with the early heat maps were just curious to see where people rode in their own town or city. But one Strava user browsing the heat maps worked for Oregon's department of transportation, and a thought struck them: could this be useful for planning bike infrastructure?

Collecting data on cycling use had previously been pretty basic, recalls Sheila Lyons, head of cycling projects at the transportation department. "It was very haphazard, two-hour counts done once a year," she says. "Volunteers, sitting on the street corner because they wanted better bike facilities. Pathetic, really."[2] Prompted by her Strava-using colleague, Lyons's team got in touch with the company and, in 2013, the department bought a year of cycling data for the state. Thus was born a spin-off business, Strava Metro.

This was all largely unexpected, explains Michael Horvath,

one of two former Harvard University rowers and relatively veteran fortysomething tech entrepreneurs who cofounded Strava in 2009. "We're not city planners," he says. "But one of the things that we learned early on is that these people just don't have very much data to begin with. Not only is ours a novel data set, in many cases it's the only data set that speaks to the behavior of cyclists in that city or region."

Strava Metro now works with around eighty places around the world, handing over data at relatively low cost— Oregon paid $20,000—or free to universities and charities. Planners in cities including Glasgow, Reykjavik, Stockholm, and Brisbane can now chart bike usage to see where lanes or other facilities might be needed, and then gauge how many more riders arrive once they're built. "It helps show the return on investment, on the tax dollars being used by authorities for things like cycle lanes," Horvath says. "They want to be able to show this was money well spent, or to learn that there was something they could have done better."[3]

The findings are not always what planners expected. In Oregon, Sheila Lyons's team found one carefully designed piece of cycle infrastructure at a busy intersection was heavily used by cyclists heading in one direction. But when riding the other way, almost all of them cut through a parking lot and a side street to avoid it. "It was an indication of an issue," Lyons says. "Bicyclists had figured out that the lane in that intersection was a bit dicey."

The Strava team themselves were initially worried that the information could be a bit skewed, as users of the app tend to be disproportionately enthusiast cyclists, who ride relatively fast—those who record the quickest time for a section of road get the title King of the Mountain. But when the files were compared to cities' manual bike counts, it turned out that once within a town or city those with Strava, typically 5 percent to 10 percent of the total riding population, take much the same routes as everyone else. "At first we weren't really sure what we had," says Shaw. "Was this just performance athletes? But what we found is that when cyclists are in the urban core they optimize for the same kind of things as everyone else. They're not trying to race across the city, they're trying to get there in one piece."

Strava holds a vast amount of information—downloading all the information for a big city like London takes two weeks—and the company is only beginning to understand what it could be used for. Innovations currently being worked on include real-time analysis of cyclist numbers for traffic planning, and the mooted ability to automatically send a warning to the phone of a driver who is approaching a Strava user on the road.

All this is not without a vested interest for the company, notes Michael Horvath: better analysis means improved bike routes, which in turn should mean more riders to download the Strava app. "We're not a philanthropy," he says. "But we are interested in the impact, what it can do in these cities to encourage people in these modes of transportation. We see that as a good return on our shareholders' investment."

Sadly, new technology and cycling are not always such a good fit. A few years ago I tried out a prototype high-tech cycling jacket in a video review on my newspaper's website. Two things were notable about this jacket. First, it was constructed from the most retina-scorching Day-Glo yellow fabric you can imagine. "It's not only the brightest thing I've ever worn, it might be the brightest thing I've ever seen," I noted, accurately, at the time.[4] But the main selling point was a series of built-in LED lights, operated via a small battery pack in a pocket. As well as flashing white lights at the front and flashing red lights at the rear, if you raised an arm to show you planned to turn, a sensor would set off some orange indicators. A satellite could probably track you from space.

This was pretty innovative at the time. The jacket has gone on to sell in the thousands and has even won awards. But watching the video again made me feel a bit depressed. It exemplifies what has become a tide of advanced products that approach cycling from entirely the wrong perspective. In this instance it is a focus on the effects of poor road safety for cyclists rather than the causes. Build decent lanes, stop cyclists having to share limited space with speeding vehicles, and suddenly a flashing, battery-operated coat seems absurdly over-the-top.

This isn't to blame the jacket manufacturer. I'm not expecting them to build bike lanes single-handedly. But I do worry that such products, in supposedly seeking to overcome the perceived dangers of cycling, in fact end up exaggerating them. As we've seen before, riding a bike in many places is less safe than it should be but is also much safer than many people believe. And so if you're a noncyclist and every bike rider you see is lit up like a particularly garish Christmas tree, the message is pretty clear: stay away.

It's notable that the company that makes the jacket I tested also manufactures specialty work wear for the construction and petrochemicals industries. These are places that are, necessarily and unavoidably, perilous at times. Cycling shouldn't be like that, and for the most part it isn't.

If you browse the various cycling-related products seeking investment on the crowdfunding website Kickstarter, it's easy to get a sense of the scale of this new industry built around a combination of poor road design and the overstatement of the perils this brings. There are cycling tops with LEDs sewn into the seams, ultrareflective beanie hats, bolt-on bike indicator lights controllable from the handlebars of your bike, even gloves with orange blinking lights. You can buy lights with combined HD cameras in case someone drives into you. These are all symptoms and exaggerations, not answers.

Elsewhere on Kickstarter you soon reach that other category of bike-related inventions: the solution in search of a problem. I somehow can't imagine I'll ever need a bike light that can receive downloads from a phone, or cycling glasses with a digital display, or a bike where you can swap between various-shaped tubes in the frame to change the feel of the ride. Yes, many such innovations are aimed more at the enthusiast, but I'm still not convinced. It all seems so overcomplicated.

That's not to say I'm a Luddite. While the very basics of a bicycle might have remained unchanged since the 1880s, new materials and inventions make modern machines astonishingly more lightweight, speedy, strong, or just about whatever you want, if you can pay for it. Should you want to ride fast or climb lots of hills, carbon fiber frames are a big advance. For those venturing farther afield, disc brakes are a revelation. Even for someone just pottering down a decent cycle lane, the experience is hugely improved by virtually puncture-proof tires and better lights. Modern bike lights are a particular revelation for anyone who began cycling in the era of clunky, brick-weight, C-sized-battery-powered behemoths which gave a pitiful yellow glow from a single incandescent bulb. Rechargeable lights now fit into a pocket, and the main issue is trying not to dazzle or hypnotize drivers with the multiple flashing LEDs.

So all praise to innovation. But sometimes the benefits come in less obvious ways—for example, the advent of barcode keys for cycle-share systems, or improved batteries in e-bikes. Elsewhere cycling can be the almost indirect beneficiary of other tech upheavals. The imminent arrival of driverless cars and automated traffic systems is likely to reshape our cities in ways we can barely imagine, but around which the bike seems likely to play a crucial role. The revolution has arrived. It's just not always the one you expected.

But How Do You Move a Fridge?

Technology also plays a big role in answering one of the most common arguments you hear against making over more of a city's road space to bikes. The point generally goes something like this: "But what about a sofa or a fridge? How do you expect to get them delivered with only bikes?" There are two responses. The first is the more obvious—no one beyond a few zealots is proposing a complete ban on trucks and vans. The other answer is perhaps a bit surprising. Some modern cargo bikes, especially those with electric assistance, are plenty big enough for a fridge, and the very biggest might even stand a chance with a sofa. Neither is necessarily what they're best at. It's mainly to stress that cycle freight is more flexible than many people believe.

E-bikes are a particularly interesting area in the way they can broaden the possibilities of cycling. As we saw in chapter 3, they can help older people stay mobile even beyond the age where they feel unable to drive. They are virtually as emission-free as a normal bike, and the way they work—the electric assist only starts up when the rider begin pedaling—relies on at least some exertion, so brings important health benefits.

It's worth quickly stressing what we mean by "e-bike." In most of Europe and the United States, these are modestly powered electric-assist machines where the motor is started by pedaling, and the powered speed is limited to about 15 to 20 mph. The situation in China and some other Asian nations is very different. Chinese cities are awash with rapid, throttle-operated, electric two-wheelers, often called e-bikes, but these are really more like electric mopeds. Their weight and speed mean they can and do intimidate, injure, or kill people. In Beijing, where there are now an estimated 2.5 million of them, electric bikes account for almost 40 percent of pedestrian injuries.

While powered bikes have been around for many decades—my grandmother used to get around her home city on a converted bicycle that had a tiny two-stroke engine attached to the back wheel—electric assistance only emerged in Japan in the 1980s. These early e-bikes tended to be expensive, with a limited range and basic batteries that needed regular replacing. Battery technology has since improved this beyond measure: some modern e-bikes can now go almost one hundred miles between charges. They are now huge business, especially in Germany and the Netherlands, where around 20 percent of all bikes sold now have electric assist.

This technology is helping drive a new type of bike-based freight business. When I visited Outspoken! Delivery, a pioneering cargo bike company in the traditionally bike-friendly English city of Cambridge, they were about to take delivery of their biggest e-cargo bike yet, a behemoth with a cargo bay almost the size of that in a small van. They let me try out what was their biggest machine at the time—a slightly smaller, electrically assisted three-wheeler. While still more or less big enough to carry that hypothetical fridge, it felt intuitive and straightforward to ride, with even the relatively small motor, meaning it was easy to start off from traffic lights.

Cycle freight also comes in smaller, more nimble forms. I watched one Outspoken! rider, Ben Cartwright, load dozens of packages into a large cargo box on a nonelectric, two-wheeled, narrow, and tandem-length machine. "It's really easy to ride," said Cartwright, who at the time had just completed a PhD in archaeology at the city's famous university.

"You get used to it pretty quickly, and it's still small enough to filter through traffic."[5] Cartwright reckoned that even with the smaller cargo bay requiring intermittent returns to base, he easily delivered more packages in a day than someone in a van.

It is in fact arguable that freight bikes could end up having as much of an impact on towns and cities as will all types of bicycle used for everyday transport. The era of Internet shopping is another technological development with likely, if inadvertent, spin-off effects for cycling. The Amazon era has left roads in many places clogged with vans delivering large numbers of laughably tiny packages that could be much more simply delivered on cargo bikes. Some see this change as inevitable. "Retail is moving online and the number of deliveries being made is going through the roof," says Sam Keam, who runs another British e-bike delivery company, ReCharge, in the seaside city of Brighton. "But there's no road space for that to happen. The only way you can grow urban economies is by changing the way you manage logistics in a city."[6]

As ever, the biggest steps are being made in more cycle-friendly nations in continental Europe. Vienna has a successful start-up business delivering healthy meals with a fleet of branded cargo bikes. One company in Prague promises its bikes can deliver a takeaway meal inside seven minutes of its being ordered.

The Swedish city of Gothenburg, meanwhile, is specifically targeting cargo bike distribution as a way to make its streets more pleasant and human-friendly. It is currently testing a strange-looking contraption called the Armadillo. With four wheels, a roof, windshield, and doors, it resembles a high-tech golf car. But under the bodywork is a lightweight metal frame and pedals, with assistance from an electric motor. This combined power helps the Armadillo tow one or more laden cargo boxes on wheels. The idea is that traditional vans and trucks take goods to a freight consolidation center on the outskirts of the city, and the Armadillo does the final mile or so. City authorities are also testing out the vehicles to carry staff like housing officers and health inspectors between appointments.

Modern cargo e-bikes are sufficiently flexible and popular that there is even an official EU-funded project, Cycle Logistics, to boost the trade. Susanne Wrighton from an Austrian think tank involved in the scheme says it's not only about convenience: "It's also a matter of more and more cities recognizing that this can really improve the quality of life for people who live in the city."[7]

Cars Are an Outdated Solution

These days, few self-respecting modern metropolises are complete without a public bike-share system. There are hundreds around the world, varying in size from about three hundred bikes (Madison, Wisconsin) to sixty-six thousand (Hangzhou, eastern China). The bikes themselves are often not hugely high-tech. The Bixi-type models pioneered in

Montreal and now also used in London and New York are vastly sturdy and feature the sort of hub-based gears and brakes which would be familiar to a 1950s cyclist, even if the built-in LED lights might surprise them a bit. But before the arrival of modern innovations to track the bikes' use and let people pay for them automatically, such systems never really had a chance to take off.

Their spiritual precursor was Amsterdam's White Bicycle movement, devised in 1965 by a small group of anarchists who acquired some donated cycles, painted them white, and left around the city, unlocked, for all to use freely. The story is chronicled by *In the City of Bikes*, a meticulously researched book about Dutch cycling culture by Pete Jordan, an Amsterdam-based US author.[8] This project was seemingly more influential for the future than useful at the time. While some living in the city then claim to have seen hundreds of white bikes in use, there were in fact never more than a few dozen, most of which were barely ridden at all and soon vanished.

According to Jordan's version the entire scheme would probably have been forgotten but for the fact that police decided to confiscate the bikes under an old law that made it illegal to leave a bicycle unlocked in the city. This in turn sparked protests during which, in a hugely Dutch detail, anarchists unscrewed the tops of metal bike bells to hurl at officers.

The organizers' aims seem nonetheless prescient in retrospect. Their manifesto, which asked in vain for city authorities to buy twenty thousand white bikes, called the car "an outdated solution." It argued: "Cars are a dangerous and totally unsuitable means of transport within the city." Even though the system itself fizzled out almost immediately, the myth gradually expanded, propagated by stunts such as someone donating a white-painted bike to John Lennon and Yoko Ono during their 1969 "bed-in" at the Amsterdam Hilton.

Lovely as such free-for-all schemes might sound, human nature appears to work against them. In the early 1990s, the local government in Cambridge, England, took fifty bikes from the police pound, painted them green, and left them at racks around the city for people to use and return. They all vanished on the first day. "It only needed one hundred people out of Cambridge's one-hundred-thousand population to foul it up," lamented Simon Sedgwick-Jell, leader of the council at the time, who was widely mocked for the idea.[9]

The one exception was La Rochelle, a small, tourist-heavy city on the west coast of France. In 1974, its mayor, Michel Crépeau—a colorful figure who held the job until his death in 1999 and once stood as a radical left candidate in the national presidential election—introduced the Vélo Jaune, or "Yellow Bicycle," scheme. These were left on racks by the harbor, for people to use and return. Amazingly, enough of them did for the system to last for decades—it still exists, but users must now show ID and pay if they keep a bike for more than two hours. The only other long-running scheme was Bycyklen in Copenhagen, which lasted from 1995 to 2012. Here, users left a twenty-kroner (about $2) coin deposit. This was the first system to use specially built bikes, without

standard-sized parts that could be easily transferred to another machine.

Even such minor successes, however, were based on significant effort—Bycyklen's system was only sustainable because
the bikes could be used in just a small part of the city center,
with police vigorously fining riders who strayed. It took the
advent of accessible digital technology for the idea to spread,
which it then did, at speed. The first such system, Vélo'v, was
introduced in the French city of Lyon in 2005, and still op-
erates. It uses a dedicated card and a PIN key to release bikes
from their docks. Two years later came Paris's Vélib', which
now has almost fifteen thousand bikes and is arguably the
system that showed how bike sharing could reshape a big
city, proving hugely popular with both locals and tourists.
Since then, progress has accelerated. Montreal's influential
Bixi system debuted in 2008, along with a pilot scheme in
Washington, DC, and the now-vast system in Hangzhou. In
2010, systems began in Mexico City and Buenos Aires, as
well as a now-very-popular one in London. New York waited
until 2013 for its Citi Bike, which has also proved a big
success. All these rely on low-key but sophisticated technology, linking bank cards or PIN keys to secure deposits
and automatically deduct fees.

And the effect has been huge. I vividly remember the
buildup to the London bike share, a project begun under one
mayor, Ken Livingstone, but launched under his successor,
Boris Johnson, meaning the machines are known universally

to Londoners as "Boris bikes." There was much skepticism before the system launched, largely based on the notion that tourists and cycling novices would climb aboard and get immediately squashed by marauding buses and trucks. That didn't happen. Instead, as tends to be the case with such systems, the Boris bikes helped to humanize the city. The bright blue machines (now red after a change of sponsor) trundle about, occasionally ridden by serious commuters or unsmiling businesspeople, but more often by families of grinning tourists, friends heading between bars, sometimes even people cycling around in the sun for the sheer fun of it. These were recognizably everyday riders.

When I interviewed Bradley Wiggins, the first Briton to win the Tour de France, he said he often uses the London bike share system when staying in the city. Wiggins said he had never at that point been recognized, let alone challenged to a sprint to the next red light, but stressed he tried to keep a low profile. "I'm quite sensible on the road, being who I am," he said. "I tend not to jump lights, I tend not to ride all over the road, or whack cars and things. Because I'll be the one in the *Daily Mail* the next day."

Dani Simons from Citi Bike in New York recalls a similar public trajectory for this system, which now regularly clocks more than fifty thousand rides a day. Initially, she says, quite a few apartment block boards objected to having docking stands nearby. This soon changed, she recalled: "You'd go back later and speak to the doormen, who became some of our best ambassadors, and they'd be showing people how to use it. It was amazing to see that shift happen so quickly. We went from a place where people were freaking out about having stations by them to one now where they're asking, 'Why can't we get a station here?' I fielded so many questions from people saying, 'Why is it here?' Now I go to parties and people just say, 'When's it coming to my neighborhood?'"

Simons argues that the system has helped cycling in the city seem more normal and everyday. "It's not just an amenity, like when a bike lane was put in it was an amenity for people who used bikes," she says. "When you talk about bike share as a piece of the public transportation infrastructure that changes it. It's not just for recreation, it's really becoming part of how people travel around. Also, you see the people using them look just like everyone else in the New York community. They're not wearing spandex or racing the wrong way down the street. They're people like you."[10]

If Anyone Tells You They Can Predict the Future, They're Lying

It seems obligatory when writing about tech-based developments to assure the reader that, whatever the dizzying pace of change so far, they've seen nothing yet. And it's the same here. As I noted in the introduction, it's one of the paradoxes of the modern story of the bicycle that such a very simple, 140-year-old design appears so adaptable and suitable to twenty-first-century life. This is, of course, particularly the case for shorter distance travel, including trips that link up people to other forms of transport.

Dr. John Zacharias, a Beijing-based academic and urban

planner who has lived in China for decades, believes cycling could make a return in the country in part through bike-share schemes, allowing people to connect to urban rail stations. "I have this feeling it's going to take off—bike sharing with metro systems," he says. "Just now the walking distances don't allow the metro systems to penetrate very far into residential districts. A bicycle-sharing system extends that by about three times."[11]

Anand Babu, meanwhile, is imagining bikes having a key role to connect with a more high-tech transport system—high-speed driverless cars. Babu, formerly head of special projects for Google, is now chief operating officer of Sidewalk Labs, a new and vastly ambitious Google spin-off that has as its modest intention to reshape cities through the conjunction of clever planning and high-tech solutions.

Sidewalk Labs has so far devised LinkNYC, a project to turn New York City's defunct pay-phone booths into digital hubs, where people can either access Wi-Fi or, if they don't have a smartphone or similar device, find information directly. Next to come is Flow, a more ambitious if so far slightly vague project, run with the US Department of Transportation, to help urban areas monitor and manage traffic and parking more effectively.

These are early days, and Babu concedes the company's urban planners occasionally have to remind its tech experts that cities prefer to change more slowly than computer systems. "I think there's a critique of technologists when they approach the domain of cities that they treat it like any other software problem," he says. "We're trying to avoid that."

Babu stresses that looking into a metaphorical crystal ball

and describing the city of the future is fraught with difficulties, so anyone who claims they can predict what will
happen in the coming few years is "probably lying." He adds:
"There are a lot of very interesting combinations of scenarios
that might unfold here." He does, however, predict that in
transport terms there are likely to be big changes in what he
calls the "20–100 mph range," taking in cars and what might
replace them, and the "10–20 mph range," covering cycling
and other short-range travel modes.

Not surprisingly for someone whose parent company is at
the forefront of developing driverless car technology, Babu
expects such creations to be in use soon. They could have a
huge and immediate impact, he believes, especially on spread-
out US cities, where some suburbs have become neglected, in
part because of the time it takes to travel to and from them.
Since existing cars would take time to be replaced, Babu says,
the near future could see lanes of freeways reserved for driverless vehicles, transporting people between distant points at
high speed. "There's a potentially transformative step-
function benefit that you can enable for people, well before
those human-driven vehicles are aged out," he explains. "As
a metro, within five to ten years you can say, anybody can get
to any point for a relatively low cost. That's a big deal."[12]

This big deal would ease pressure on crowded inner cities.
The moment people can get from a suburb rapidly, reliably,
and at low cost, these suddenly become far more attractive,
for both living and businesses. In turn, the gradual demise of
private cars would make the suburbs more walkable and
bikeable, and thus increasingly pleasant places to live.

How would this happen? As with bike schemes, it would be through sharing. One of the big appeals of automated cars for technologists is that they have the potential to be much more efficient than the current, human-driven variants. Even if you're a regular driver, chances are your car spends 90 percent or more of its time sitting idle outside your home or in a parking space elsewhere. Car club systems do exist, but it still involves making sure your local vehicle is free, walking to the designated parking spot and driving off. Self-driven cars, the futurists believe, could be like a universal and less exploitative version of Uber—the click of an app summons the nearest free automated car. No more private cars—and this is the big hypothetical step—could see the number of vehicles in most cities fall to 10 percent or 15 percent of what it is now. Bingo—lots more space in which to move, and to live, and to cycle.

Where precisely does the bike fit into this brave new world? Babu believes there is "tremendous latent demand" for people to live in communities based around walking and cycling, something currently thwarted by the sheer number of cars. Thus, as he sees it, the modern suburb (or inner city) would see people hop onto a bike for local trips, or to get to the next, more rapid form of transport. "You could potentially move to a model where these suburban cities, which were so reliant on individual vehicles, could become incredibly well-connected metropolitan areas, where you could get anywhere within thirty minutes, plus a first mile/last mile of walking or bike connection," he says. "You're in a high-speed, shared-vehicle majority of miles, but then the last mile or first mile you embrace a wide amount of innovation around all sorts of personal vehicles, whether self-powered or electric powered, to connect."

It might seem a bit far-fetched, this slightly *Truman Show* vision of quiet, picket-fence suburbs, the roads populated by commuters pedaling or whirring past on bikes and e-bikes to connect with a twenty-minute dash to the office. But driverless technology is already here. Car insurance premiums are predicted to plummet in the next couple of years as existing crash-avoidance and sensor-triggered braking systems become more widespread, eliminating many of the everyday bangs, bumps, and scrapes that have for decades been part of urban driving.

Similarly, you might be a touch wary about a tech behemoth like Google supposedly taking an interest in cycling. Bikes are fairly basic things, for the most part. But they can and do appeal to the technology industry, in part because they are so efficient and adaptable, characteristics the tech sector sees as its own. This is not just theory. In 2015, Google announced plans to try and ease terrible road congestion around its headquarters in Mountain View, California, by getting together with the local county government to plan and build a network of useable and safe bike lanes. The initiative started, Babu explains, after Google and other local employers did a study of car commute patterns and found 20 to 30 percent of trips were under five miles, perfectly achievable on a bike, especially given the agreeable local climate.

"They're now embarking on a really aggressive campaign that involves dedicated bike lanes, subsidized bikes, and e-bikes, targeting that population," Babu says. "It will take away road real estate from others in some cases. However, if you can move that many trips to more effective mechanisms like bikes, it unblocks everyone else. That's how they're starting to message the trade-off—if you can move these shorter distance trips to bicycles, yes, in some cases you're taking road space, but that benefits the remaining drivers significantly."

Slightly less promising, from my point of view, is another prediction from Babu: that the fast-falling cost of carbon fiber could allow the rapid construction of elevated bike superhighways, which could even be translucent. "We think there's a model within the next five to ten years where you can do extremely low-cost, very, very lightweight, small-footprint elevated bike paths," he says. As I mentioned in chapter 5, I'm not especially a fan of such plans to remove cyclists from the streets, however well intentioned. Cycling is not just about people getting around. It's about them stopping, interacting, shopping, mixing. Being human, in other words.

I can, however, forgive this of Sidewalk Labs. In a strange sort of way, these grandiose dreams of carbon fiber bike flyovers are oddly reassuring. Why? Because it shows the people who are likely to reshape our cities are thinking about cycling. And this wasn't always the case.

Think back fifty or more years to when the predecessors

of Babu and his colleagues, in this case municipal planners, were cutting miles of urban freeways through city centers. These were people like Robert Moses, the "master builder" of New York City, whose automobile-dominated idea of urban life was hugely influential both across the US and elsewhere.

His British near-equivalent was Professor Colin Buchanan, commissioned by the government in the early 1960s to investigate what could be done to stop towns and cities being choked by motor vehicles, the number of which had doubled in a decade. Buchanan's eventual report, 1963's *Traffic in Towns*, became something of a sensation, even being published as a paperback book that remains in print.

Buchanan, a civil engineer and town planner, was by no means a disciple of the car, once describing motor traffic as a "destructive lava, welling out from the towns, searing and scorching in long channels, and ever-ready to invade new areas." His report was notable in part because it warned that urban dwellers would not accept unlimited amounts of vehicles among them, given the impact this would have on people's lives. "We are nourishing at great cost a monster of great potential destructiveness," he wrote vividly.[13]

But for all this, Buchanan clearly saw no alternative to the private car. His report was based entirely around ways to cope with more motor traffic, not whether there was a way to avoid it. This is not to Buchanan's personal discredit. It was the era when more or less every arm of government was planning for a car-based future. Also in 1963 came an official report into Britain's still-huge rail network by another famous technocrat, Sir Richard Beeching, which saw almost a third of the country's rural train lines ripped up.

But it is nonetheless notable to compare Buchanan's vision of the future with that of Babu's when it comes to cycling. "It would be very expensive, and probably impracticable, to build a completely separate system of tracks for cyclists," Buchanan wrote after briefly considering how bikes could fit into the new era of roads. Looking ahead to a hypothetical future, he added: "It must be admitted that it is a moot point how many cyclists there will be in 2010."

Buchanan was one of many bureaucrats and politicians in that era to write off the bike. But it is a persistent, adaptable creation. And now, it seems, the bicycle's time has come again.

The Future Is Here

"The Car Will Become an Accessory to the Smartphone"

In his book *Roads Were Not Built for Cars,* the British writer Carlton Reid explores the fascinating story of how, in the late nineteenth century, it was mainly cycling organizations that led the lobbying for properly paved highways. With the popularity of the bicycle predating any real use of cars by decades, groups like the League of American Bicyclists and, in the UK, the Cyclists' Touring Club (CTC) were influential in pushing for many of the roads that still exist today, largely so their members could ride in more comfort and at greater speed.

Reid has described the book as "revisionism with an agenda," describing his agenda thus: "I want motorists to think before they say or think, 'Get off the road, roads are for cars.'"[1] It is a laudable ambition. That said, what fascinates me most in the story is less the way this all happened than how little time it took.

In the mid-1890s, bikes ruled the roads. As late as July 1896, the CTC was still debating whether it should admit the "horseless carriage movement," seen more as a curiosity rather than a threat. Cars in Britain remained limited to a maximum speed of 5 mph and had to be preceded by someone carrying a red flag. But in November 1896, that rule was abolished, and everything began to change.

The new law, which followed vehement lobbying by the fledgling auto industry, saw speed limits raised to 14 mph, a velocity still gauged against the limitations of a horse. This soon became 20 mph, then no limit at all. Within three decades there were 2.5 million motor vehicles on the roads and more than seven thousand people being killed a year. The interloper had triumphed.

It seems likely that another road transport revolution is about to hit us, undoing the decades of undisputed dominance for the motor vehicle. This time it won't be a straightforward swap. Instead, a predicted steady decline in car use will see it supplanted by a range of transport options, everything from the automated driverless vehicles we heard about in the previous chapter to trams and metro rail systems. And in many urban areas the vacuum for shorter trips could be filled by a combination of walking and cycling.

This might sound like so much wishful thinking, and I admit I'm no neutral pundit. But it's already happening. In 2015, Oslo, the Norwegian capital, announced plans to completely ban private cars from its compact city center within four years, in part to reduce greenhouse gas emissions.[2] Stockholm in Sweden has mooted a similar idea.[3] The Finnish capital, Helsinki, has outlined an ambitious plan to not so much bar cars from the city center as make them pointless, thanks to a proposed "mobility on demand" system, taking in shared bikes, driverless cars, buses, and other means, all organized via one app.[4]

It will not just be a Nordic utopia. Lyon, birthplace of the modern bike-share system, is plotting to extend its Vélo'v cycle network to electric cars and other communal means of transport. Gilles Vesco, the Lyon politician responsible for sustainable transport, talks in grand, ambitious terms. "Digital information is the fuel of mobility," he told a colleague of mine in an interview. "Some transport sociologists say that information about mobility is 50 percent of mobility. The car will become an accessory to the smartphone."[5]

All this can feel almost inconceivable for the great majority of people who have only ever lived in a world where motor vehicles were just about the only choice for personal travel. But much as the cycling groups were taken unawares by the car, it could all be coming much more quickly than we expect.

A Copernican Revolution in Transport

How quickly? The first person I asked was Klaus Bondam, head of the Danish cycling union and formerly Copenhagen's mayor for roads and infrastructure. Nearing the end of my long chat in his office, I asked him how he saw the city changing in the coming years. The answer was illuminating. "Look at something like car parking," he said. "It's so old-fashioned in my eyes. The private ownership of a car—that will end in the next ten to fifteen years. I think it's going to be a combination of shared cars, of city cars, of public transport, bicycles, electric bicycles, of freight distribution by electric cargo bikes."

This sounded like a rapid timetable, I said—would the end of the private car really come within such a time? He was adamant: "I'm totally convinced about that," he said. "Why on earth would you make a big investment that you just leave outside ninety-five percent of the time and don't use it?"[6]

We were in Copenhagen, of course, a city with comprehensive bike and transit infrastructure, where cars are already restricted in some central areas. But as I talked to other people, everyone from city planners, to advocates, to mayors to Olympic champions, I asked them the same question about their cities and transport and the answers were uncannily similar.

Boris Johnson, speaking a week before the end of his term as London mayor and about to return to national politics, told me he was proud of having doubled bike use during eight years in office. But his hope, Johnson explained, was that London could see the current 3 percent or so of trips made by bicycle shoot up to 20 percent. This was, he agreed, "a big ask" but very possible. Typically for him, Johnson phrased the serious intent within a joke. "It was twenty percent in 1904," he said. "What's the point of being a conservative if you can't turn the clock back to 1904? That's what I want to know."[7]

Soon afterward, I interviewed Bradley Wiggins, Britain's most-successful-ever racing cyclist. Noting the newly built separated bike lanes just opening in London, Wiggins predicted that the UK could soon see Dutch levels of bike use. "Cyclists aren't going to go away," he said. "As the issues grow with cars, and emissions, and all these things, and roads getting busier, cycling is only going to get more popular, become more of a means of transport. People are aware at the moment that there is a boom in cycling. But as that boom becomes the norm and twenty years pass, we may get to a stage where we're like an Amsterdam. I can't see it not happening, to be honest."

New York City has already vastly increased the provision for cyclists in recent years. Janette Sadik-Khan, who oversaw much of that change as the city's transport commissioner for more than six years, is also among those who believe much more is to come. "Transportation is almost going through a Copernican revolution," she said. "There's a tremendous change in understanding that our streets are incredible assets, and that they've been underutilized for generations. The potential is really hidden in plain sight."[8]

Paul Steely White of the Transportation Alternatives advocacy group predicts an "exponential increase in cycling ridership and volumes," fueled by new lanes, a growing Citi Bike network, and the rise of new technologies.

"E-bikes are going to make it a lot more accessible," he said. "There are a lot of people in New York who just don't want to bike over the bridges—they're a fairly steep hill for some folk. And some people might be wearing a three-piece suit and don't want to get sweaty. There's going to be a confluence of making it much safer, the bikes becoming easier and more comfortable for people to use."

He thinks Klaus Bondam's prediction for Copenhagen could hold true for New York, he said: "I have a friend who says driving in city centers will become like smoking in public restaurants in fifteen or twenty years. There's only so much street space to go around, and we can't build ourselves out of that political conundrum. We tried that, and it didn't work. That means higher capacity modes have to rule the roost."[9]

The Future Is Here

Those quoted above are experts in their area, but they're also people with an interest, and often a vested interest, in cycling. They might be expected to say what they do. Such unanimity about a predicted bike-centric future must come with qualifiers and caveats. That said, the more I've looked into the case for mass cycling while writing this book, the more compelling the evidence seems.

If, indeed, the cars do gradually begin to empty out of our towns and cities and we see a much-increased role for bikes, along with walking and public transport, there are immeasurable benefits, for all the many, compelling reasons outlined in the preceding pages. It's worth noting that many of these positives don't emerge if we only embrace the more passive new technologies and ignore everything else. The driverless cars of the near future might not crash or get caught in jams, but they will do nothing to stem the pandemic of illness caused by sedentary lives. And if they alone predominate, our cities risk becoming even more impersonal. Without even a driver to connect with, there are just passengers—barely glimpsed through glass, sealed, uncommunicative, and anonymous within a speeding capsule.

In contrast, more bikes means more people enjoying good health for longer. The economy gets a notable boost, not least from not having to pay out quite so much to treat the many, expensive ailments linked to sedentary living. Air quality improves, road casualties fall, and a small but notable step is taken toward mitigating the worst consequences of runaway climate change.

But, arguably as important, streets suddenly become based around people who, while moving, are recognizably, obviously, reassuringly human.

I've spent much of this book focusing on the societal reasons for getting people on two wheels. But in many ways the most powerful arguments come when you bring it down to the individual. At risk of sounding borderline messianic, cycling makes your life better. My history with the bicycle is, admittedly, a particular one. Not everyone will credit the bike with transforming them from a wheezing, fragile teenager into

someone newly imbued with a joyous sense of their physicality. But the trajectory could be equally transformative for
many people. If it's not asthma it could be diabetes, heart
disease, or obesity that could be tackled or prevented.

There's yet more to it. Riding a bike keeps me in touch
with the weather, makes me feel firsthand the grip of the
changing seasons. The importance and impact of this is not
to be underestimated. An innovative Danish charity called
Cycling Without Age uses volunteers to take older people too
frail to use a bike themselves for rides on cycle rickshaws. Its
motto sums up one of the joys of cycling: "Everyone has the
right to wind in their hair." This sounds more evocative still
in the original Danish: "*Alle har ret til vind i håret.*" This is a
pure joy that never tires. It can't be stressed enough that
without decent cycling infrastructure, this is precisely what
the majority of people are denied, especially the more vulnerable or delicate, who don't want to or can't brave the
traffic.

Cycling is also by far the best way to get to know a town
or city, fast enough to cover a lot of ground, but sufficiently
sedate and open that you can take in what's there, stare
through shop fronts, observe the gradual ascent of new
buildings, lament the disappearance of old ones, smile at tod-
dlers, wave to someone you know. In somewhere as large and
traffic-choked as London, a bike has a near-magical ability to
get me precisely where I want to be to within a minute or two
of when I expected, and with a smile on my face. Yes, public
transport has a huge role, as do the other noncar alternatives
on the horizon. But in an era of unprecedented urbanization,

the bike has an unparalleled capacity to work with the streets, not fight against them, to complement humans, not seal them away or make them suddenly a mortal danger to others.

I'll leave the last word to the person who, of all the activists and politicians we have encountered in this book, faces arguably the biggest and most thankless task. Jack Yabut, whom we met in chapter 6, is the longstanding head of the main cycling lobby group in Manila, the car-dominated capital of the Philippines. I asked Yabut why his organization has the beautifully evocative name of the Firefly Brigade. His answer, for me, sums up perfectly why bikes are needed and why, in many places, they are returning in numbers not seen for decades.

"It came from some friends who shared the idea that the first thing that disappears from a city's landscape because of the pollution are the fireflies," Yabut told me. "We believe that if we can help to clean up the air, the land and water quality, then the fireflies can come back. And the vehicle, the instrument to do it, is the bicycle. It's something that can answer so many problems.

"We're just a volunteer organization, doing what we can. But we're like the fireflies: we're the smallest particles in the equation, but we believe that we put everything together. And then we end up as a swarm. That's when everything starts to change."[10]

Around the globe this most benign of swarms is here. On their own, each cyclist is just flesh, blood, and a machine of such beguiling simplicity and perfection that its fundamentals have stayed roughly the same for 140 years. But together, like the fireflies, they are a powerful indicator of the vitality and livability of a city's streets. Together they can save the world.

INTRODUCTION

1 Department for Transport, *National Travel Survey: England 2015*, 2016, https://www.gov.uk/government/uploads/system /uploads/attachment_data/file/551437/national-travel-survey -2015.pdf.

2 Ministry of Transport, Public Works and Water Management, *Cycling in the Netherlands*, 2009, http://www.fietsberaad.nl /library/repository/bestanden/CyclingintheNetherlands2009 .pdf.

3 United Nations, "World's Population Increasingly Urban with More Than Half Living in Urban Areas," July 10, 2014, http://www.un.org/en/development/desa/news/population /world-urbanization-prospects-2014.html.

CHAPTER 1

1 Royal College of Physicians, "National Review of Asthma Deaths," 2015, https://www.rcplondon.ac.uk/projects /national-review-asthma-deaths.

2 Daniela Schmid and Michael F. Leitzmann, "Television Viewing and Time Spent Sedentary in Relation to Cancer Risk: A Meta-Analysis," *Journal of the National Cancer Institute* 106, Vol. 7 (2014), http://jnci.oxfordjournals.org /content/106/7/dju098.full.pdf+html.

3   Interview with the author.

4   John Pucher and Ralph Buehler, "At the Frontiers of Cycling: Policy Innovations in the Netherlands, Denmark, and Germany," *World Transport Policy and Practice* (December 2007), https://ralphbu.files.wordpress.com/2015/03/frontiers.pdf.

5   Jeroen Johan de Hartog, Hanna Boogaard, Hans Nijland, and Gerard Hoek, "Do the Health Benefits of Cycling Outweigh the Risks?" *Environmental Health Perspectives* 118 (2010):1109–16, http://ehp.niehs.nih.gov/0901747.

6   Pedestrian and Bicycle Information Center, "Pedestrian and Bicyclist Crash Statistics," http://www.pedbikeinfo.org/data/factsheet_crash.cfm.

7   K. Powell and S. Blair, "The Public Health Burdens of Sedentary Living Habits: Theoretical but Realistic Estimates," *Medicine & Science in Sports & Exercise* 26, Vol. 7 (1994): 851–6, doi: 10.1249/00005768-199407000-00007.

8   British Heart Foundation, "Physical Activity Statistics 2012," July 2012, https://www.bhf.org.uk/-/media/files/research/heart-statistics/m130-bhf_physical-activity-supplement_2012.pdf.

9   Gov.uk, "Casualties Involved in Reported Road Accidents," updated June 30, 2016, https://www.gov.uk/government/statistical-data-sets/ras30-reported-casualties-in-road-accidents#table-ras30065.

10 Interview with the author.

11 Interview with the author.

12 World Health Organization, "Physical Inactivity: A Global Public Health Problem," 2016, http://www.who.int/diet physicalactivity/factsheet_inactivity/en.

13   I. M. Lee et al., "Effect of physical inactivity on major non-communicable diseases worldwide: An analysis of burden of disease and life expectancy," *The Lancet* 380 (2012):219–29.

14   Interview with the author.

15   Charles E. Matthews et al., "Influence of Exercise, Walking, Cycling, and Overall Nonexercise Physical Activity on Mortality in Chinese Women," *American Journal of Epidemiology* 165, Vol. 12 (2007):1343–50.

16   Interview with the author.

17   Interview with the author.

18   World Health Organization, "The Challenge of Obesity—Quick Statistics," http://www.euro.who.int/en/health-topics/noncommunicable-diseases/obesity/data-and-statistics.

19   Department for Transport, "National Travel Survey: England 2014," September 2, 2015, https://www.gov.uk/government/uploads/system/uploads/attachment_data/file/457752/nts 2014-01.pdf.

20   Interview with the author.

21   Interview with the author.

22   Press Association, "Obesity Bigger Cost for Britain Than War and Terror," November 20, 2014, https://www.the guardian.com/society/2014/nov/20/obesity-bigger-cost-than -war-and-terror.

23   National Health Executive, "Obesity Will Bankrupt NHS If Unchecked—Stevens," September 18, 2014, http://www.nationalhealthexecutive.com/Health-Care-News/obesity -will-bankrupt-nhs-if-unchecked--stevens.

24   Interview with the author.

25   Ulf Ekelund et al., "Physical Activity and All-cause Mortality across Levels of Overall and Abdominal Adiposity in

European Men and Women: The European Prospective Investigation into Cancer and Nutrition Study," *The American Journal of Clinical Nutrition* (2015), http://dx.doi.org/10.3945/ajcn.114.100065.

26   A. Colin Bell et al., "The Road to Obesity or the Path to Prevention: Motorized Transportation and Obesity in China," *Obesity Research* 10, Vol. 4 (2002):277–83, http://www.cpc.unc.edu/projects/nutrans/publications/ColinRoadOR.pdf.

27   Interview with the author.

28   Interview with the author.

29   Office for National Statistics, "2011 Census Analysis—Method of Travel to Work in England and Wales Report," February 13, 2013, http://www.ons.gov.uk/ons/rel/census/2011-census-analysis/method-of-travel-to-work-in-england-and-wales/art-method-of-travel-to-work.html.

30   Interview with the author.

31   Interview with the author.

32   Alexander Kennedy, "Exercise and Heart Disease: Cardiac Findings in Fatal Cycle Accidents," *British Journal of Sports Medicine* 31 (1997):328–31.

33   Lars Bo Andersen et al., "All-Cause Mortality Associated with Physical Activity During Leisure Time, Work, Sports, and Cycling to Work," *Archives of Internal Medicine* 160 (2000):1621–8.

34   Royal College of Physicians, "Consultant Physicians Working with Patients," 2013, https://www.rcplondon.ac.uk/file/1578/download?token=w0PgEBDD.

35   David R. Bassett Jr. et al., "Walking, Cycling, and Obesity Rates in Europe, North America, and Australia," *Journal of Physical Activity and Health* 5 (2008):795–814, http://www.cycle-helmets.com/walk-bike-obesity-rates.pdf.

36   Interview with the author.

37   Interview with the author.

38   Interview with the author.

39   Interview with the author.

40   Interview with the author.

41   Hiekki Karppanen and Eero Mervaala, "Sodium Intake and Hypertension," *Progress in Cardiovascular Diseases* 49, Vol. 2 (2006):59–75, http://dx.doi.org/10.1016/j.pcad.2006.07.001.

42   Interview with the author.

43   Interview with the author.

44   Interview with the author.

CHAPTER 2

1   Interview with the author.

2   Association for Safe International Road Travel, "Annual Global Road Crash Statistics," http://asirt.org/initiatives /informing-road-users/road-safety-facts/road-crash-statistics.

3   Vic Langenhoff, "Stop de Kindermoord," *De Tidj*, September 20, 1972. Translation from Dutch by Mark Wagenbuur.

4   Interview with the author.

5   Fietsberaad, "Cycling in the Netherlands," 2009, http://www .fietsberaad.nl/library/repository/bestanden/Cyclinginthe Netherlands2009.pdf.

6   Figure from Fietsersbond (Dutch cycling union).

7   Statistics Netherlands, "Traffic Death Toll Substantially Down in 2013," April 24, 2014, https://www.cbs.nl/en-gb /news/2014/17/traffic-death-toll-substantially-down-in-2013.

8   Interview with the author.

9   All Party Parliamentary Cycling Group, "Get Britain
     Cycling," April 2013, https://allpartycycling.files.wordpress
     .com/2013/04/get-britain-cycling_goodwin-report.pdf.

10   Colin G. Pooley, "Understanding Walking and Cycling,"
     2011, http://www.its.leeds.ac.uk/fileadmin/user_upload
     /UWCReportSept2011.pdf.

11   Rachel Aldred et al., "Cycling Near Misses: Findings from
     Year One of the Near Miss Project," 2015, http://www
     .nearmiss.bike/wp-content/uploads/2014/12/Nearmissreport
     -final-web-2.pdf.

12   Rachel Aldred, "Cycling Near Misses: 'You Need Ceaseless
     Vigilance If You Want to Stay Alive,'" *The Guardian*, March
     24, 2015, https://www.theguardian.com/cities/2015/mar/24
     /cycling-near-miss-close-pass-road-rage.

13   Julia Jones and Eve Brower, "American Deaths in Terrorism
     vs. Gun Violence in One Graph," CNN.com, December 30,
     2015, http://www.cnn.com/2015/10/02/us/oregon-shooting
     -terrorism-gun-violence.

14   Author's tally of CDC statistics.

15   Gerd Gigerenzer, "Dread Risk, September 11, and Fatal
     Traffic Accidents," *Psychological Science* 15, Vol. 4 (2004):
     286–7, https://www.mpib-berlin.mpg.de/volltexte/institut
     /dok/full/gg/GG_Dread_2004.pdf.

16   Robert Davis, *Death on the Streets: Cars and the Mythology
     of Road Safety* (West Yorkshire, England: Leading Edge
     Press & Publishing Ltd), 1991, p. 41.

17   Simon Rogers, "Mortality Statistics: Every Cause of Death in
     England and Wales," *The Guardian*, January 14, 2011,
     https://www.theguardian.com/news/datablog/2011/jan/14
     /mortality-statistics-causes-death-england-wales-2009.

18   NHTSA National Center for Statistics and Analysis, "Distracted Driving 2013," April 2015, http://www .distraction.gov/downloads/pdfs/Distracted_Driving_2013 _Research_note.pdf.

19   National Highway Traffic Safety Administration, "NHTSA Survey Finds 660,000 Drivers Using Cell Phones or Manipulating Electronic Devices While Driving at Any Given Daylight Moment," April 5, 2013, http://www.nhtsa.gov /About+NHTSA/Press+Releases/NHTSA+Survey+Finds +660,000+Drivers+Using+Cell+Phones+or+Manipulating+ Electronic+Devices+While+Driving+At+Any+Given+Daylight +Moment.

20   Interview with the author.

21   Peter Walker, "80mph Speed Limit 'Would Increase Deaths by 20%,'" *The Guardian*, December 25, 2011, https://www .theguardian.com/uk/2011/dec/25/80mph-speed-limit -increase-deaths.

22   Fred Mannering, "An Empirical Analysis of Driver Perceptions of the Relationship . . .," *Transportation Research Part F* (2008), https://engineering.purdue.edu/~flm /CE361_files/Mannering-TRF-08.pdf.

23   Grant Rollins, "Speed Cams Pull a Fast One," *The Sun*, September 30, 2015, https://www.thesun.co.uk/archives /news/190904/speed-cams-pull-a-fast-one.

24   J. S. Dean, *Murder Most Foul* (London: George Allen & Unwin Ltd), 1947. Full text available: http://www.oxpa.org .uk/docs/Murder%20most%20foul.pdf.

25   Ibid.

26   Ibid.

27   Mayer Hillman et al., *One False Move. A Study of Children's Independent Mobility* (London: Policy Studies Institute),

1990, http://john-adams.co.uk/wp-content/uploads/2007/11/one%20false%20move.pdf.

28   Ibid.

29   Ibid.

30   Peter Jacobsen et al., "Who Owns the Roads? How Motorised Traffic Discourages Walking and Cycling," *Injury Prevention* 15 (2009):369–73, http://dx.doi.org/10.1136/ip.2009.022566.

31   Interview with the author.

32   Nathan Tempey, "NYPD: Despite What We Said Earlier, Cyclist Killed in Brooklyn Wasn't Salmoning After All," Gothamist.com, April 26, 2016, http://gothamist.com/2016/04/26/hit-and-run_lauren_davis_update.php.

33   Miranda Katz, "NYPD Says It's Possible Truck's 'Wind Force' Killed Park Slope Cyclist," Gothamist.com, April 21, 2016, http://gothamist.com/2016/04/21/wind_force_cyclist_truck.php.

34   Ian Roberts and Carolyn Coggan, "Blaming Children for Child Pedestrian Injuries," *Social Science and Medicine* 38 (1994):749–53, http://dx.doi.org/10.1016/0277-9536(94)90465-0.

35   Martin Porter, "Dangerous Drivers Should Not Be Allowed to Choose Trial by Jury," *The Guardian*, April 8, 2016.

36   Tamsyn Kent, "Cycling Deaths: Fewer Than Half of Drivers Face Jail, BBC.com, July 20, 2014, http://www.bbc.co.uk/newsbeat/article/28345522/cycling-deaths-fewer-than-half-of-drivers-face-jail.

37   BBC, "Motorists Still Driving Despite Many Penalty Points, Figures Show," September 5, 2013, http://www.bbc.com.b.tldw.me/news/uk-politics-23967547.

38   A. Lightstone et al., "Relationship Between Driver's Record and Automobile versus Child Pedestrian Collisions," *Injury Prevention* 3 (1997):262–66, http://injuryprevention.bmj .com/content/3/4/262.full.pdf.

39   Ronald M. Davis, "Accidents Are Not Unpredictable," *British Medical Journal* (June 2001) 322:1320.

40   Department for Transport, "Relationship between Speed and Risk of Fatal Injury: Pedestrians and Car Occupants," September 2010, http://nacto.org/docs/usdg/relationship _between_speed_risk_fatal_injury_pedestrians_and_car _occupants_richards.pdf.

41   Brian C. Tefft, "Impact Speed and a Pedestrian's Risk of Severe Injury or Death," September 2011, https://www.aaa foundation.org/sites/default/files/2011PedestrianRiskVs Speed.pdf.

42   OECD statistics.

43   UK Department for Transport statistics.

44   Interview with the author.

45   Interview with the author.

CHAPTER 3

1   Peter Walker, "Utrecht's Cycling Lessons for Migrants: 'Riding a Bike Makes Me Feel More Dutch,'" *The Guardian*, April 28, 2016, https://www.theguardian.com/cities/2016 /apr/28/utrecht-cycling-lessons-refugees-riding-bike-feel -dutch.

2   Interview with the author.

3   UK Office for National Statistics.

4   Center for Transit Oriented Development, 2008 study.

5   2011 UK census, car or van availability by local authority.

6   Enrique Peñalosa TED talk, September 2013. http://www
.ted.com/talks/enrique_penalosa_why_buses_represent
_democracy_in_action.

7   UK National Travel Survey.

8   League of American Bicyclists.

9   John Pucher and Ralph Buehler, *City Cycling* (Cambridge,
MA: The MIT Press), 2012.

10   2011 census, analysis: cycling to work.

11   Pucher and Buehler, *City Cycling.*

12   TransAlt, "Fifth and Sixth Avenue Bicycle and Traffic Study,"
2015, https://www.transalt.org/sites/default/files/news
/reports/2015/TransAlt_5th_6th_Avenue_Report.pdf.

13   Rosamund Urwin, "Why Are Female Cyclists More
Vulnerable to London's Lorries?" *Evening Standard*, June 24,
2015, http://www.standard.co.uk/lifestyle/london-life/why
-women-seem-to-be-more-vulnerable-around-traffic
-blackspots-in-london-10341420.html.

14   Steve Connor, "Professor Steve Jones: A Very Natural
Scientist," *Independent*, April 10, 1999, http://www
.independent.co.uk/voices/profile-professor-steve-jones-a
-very-natural-scientist-1086633.html.

15   Patricia A. Vertinsky, *The Eternally Wounded Woman*
(Champaign: The University of Illinois Press), 1994.

16   Interview with the author.

17   Chris Rissel et al., "Two Pilot Studies of the Effect of
Bicycling on Balance and Leg Strength among Older Adults,"
Journal of Environmental and Public Health, Vol. 2013,
http://dx.doi.org/10.1155/2013/686412.

18   AARP, "Waiting for a Ride: Transit Access and America's Aging Population," 2012, http://www.aarp.org/content/dam /aarp/livable-communities/learn/transportation/waiting-for -a-ride-transit-access-and-americas-aging-population-aarp .pdf.

19   Jack Oortwijn, "Dutch E-bikes Excel in Growing Bicycle Sales," *Bike Europe*, February 2, 2016, http://www.bike-eu .com/sales-trends/nieuws/2015/11/e-bikes-excel-in-growing -bicycle-sales-10124772.

20   Interview with the author.

21   Odense municipality statistic.

22   National Center for Safe Routes to School, "How Children Get to School," November 2011, http://saferoutesinfo.org /sites/default/files/resources/NHTS_school_travel_report _2011_0.pdf.

23   Department for Transport: National Travel Survey.

24   Alison Carver et al., "A Comparison Study of Children's Independent Mobility in England and Australia," *Children's Geographies* 11, Vol. 4 (2013):461–75, http://dx.doi.org/10.1 080/14733285.2013.812303.

25   Alison Carver et al, "Bicycles Gathering Dust Rather Than Raising Dust—Prevalence and Predictors of Cycling among Australian Schoolchildren," *Journal of Science and Medicine in Sport* 18 (2015):540–44, http://dx.doi.org/10.1016/j.jsams .2014.07.004.

26   Alison Carver et al., "Are Children and Adolescents Less Active If Parents Restrict Their Physical Activity and Active Transport Due to Perceived Risk?" *Social Science & Medicine* 70 (2010):1799–1805, http://dx.doi.org/10.1016/j .socscimed.2010.02.010.

27   Interview with the author.

28   Interview with the author.

29   "What are the barriers to cycling amongst ethnic minority groups and people from deprived backgrounds?" November 2011, http://content.tfl.gov.uk/barriers-to-cycling-for-ethnic-minorities-and-deprived-groups-summary.pdf.

30   Greater London Authority, "Human Streets: The Mayor's Vision for Cycling, Three Years on," March 2016, https://www.london.gov.uk/sites/default/files/human_streets_0.pdf.

31   Interview with the author.

32   Brian McKenzie, "Modes Less Traveled—Bicycling and Walking to Work in the United States: 2008–2012," May 2014, https://www.census.gov/prod/2014pubs/acs-25.pdf.

33   Interview with the author.

34   Interview with the author.

35   OECD, "Launch of OECD Report—The Cost of Air Pollution: Health Impacts of Road Transport," May 21, 2014, http://www.oecd.org/about/secretary-general/launch-of-oecd-report-the-cost-of-air-pollution-health-impacts-of-road-transport.htm.

36   World Health Organization, Global Health Observatory data.

37   Steve Yim and Steven Barrett, "Public Health Impacts of Combustion Emissions in the United Kingdom," *Environmental Science and Technology* 26 (2012):4291–96.

38   Peter Walker, "Air Pollution: How Big a Problem Is It for Cyclists?" *The Guardian*, February 20, 2014, https://www.theguardian.com/environment/bike-blog/2014/feb/20/air-pollution-cyclists-bike-blog.

39   WHO Global Urban Ambient Air Pollution Database.

40   2011 Indian census, quoted by United Nations Economic Programme.

41   Gordon Mitchell and Danny Dorling, "An Environmental
      Justice Analysis of British Air Quality," *Environment and
      Planning* (2003):909–29, http://www.dannydorling.org/wp
      -content/files/dannydorling_publication_id1827.pdf.

42   Katie King and Sean Healy, "Analysing Air Pollution
      Exposure in London," https://www.london.gov.uk/sites
      /default/files/analysing_air_pollution_exposure_in_london
      _-_technical_report_-_2013.pdf.

43   Walker, "Air Pollution: How Big a Problem Is It for
      Cyclists?"

44   Greater London Authority, "Mayor of London Announces
      Bold Plans to Clean Up London's Toxic Air," May 13, 2016,
      https://www.london.gov.uk/press-releases/mayoral/bold
      -plans-to-clean-up-londons-toxic-air.

45   Interview with the author.

46   European Commission Joint Research Centre: C02 per capita
      for world countries.

47   Climate Reality Project.

48   European Cyclists' Federation, "Cycle More Often 2 Cool
      Down the Planet," November 2011, https://ecf.com/sites/ecf
      .com/files/co2%20study.pdf.

49   Jacob Mason, Lew Fulton, and Zane McDonald, "A Global
      High Shift Cycling Scenario," November 12, 2015, https://
      www.itdp.org/wp-content/uploads/2015/11/A-Global-High
      -Shift-Cycling-Scenario_Nov-2015.pdf.

50   Interview with the author.

51   Interview with the author.

CHAPTER 4

1   Interview with the author.

2   Odense municipality figures.

3   Interview with the author.

4   Chris Kenyon, "Unilever PLC, with €50bn Turnover and 1,200 Staff in London, Backs 'Crossrail for Bikes,'" CyclingWorks.com, October 6, 2014, https://cyclingworks .wordpress.com/2014/10/06/unilever.

5   Peter Walker, "Cyclists v Lobbyists: Gloves Are off in the Battle for London's Cycle Lanes," *The Guardian*, October 10, 2014, https://www.theguardian.com/world/2014/oct/10 /cyclists-lobbyists-battle-london-cycle-lanes-boris-johnson.

6   Interview with the author.

7   David Carslaw, "Oxford Street—Highest NO2 Concentrations in the World?" LondonAir.org, July 9, 2014, http://www.londonair.org.uk/london/asp/news.asp?NewsId =OxfordStHighNO2.

8   Reuven Blau, "Mike Bloomberg Vetoes 'Living Wage' Bill," *New York Daily News*, May 31, 2012, http://www.nydaily news.com/news/politics/mike-bloomberg-vetoes-living -wage-bill-article-1.1087901

9   Interview with the author.

10   "Shoppers and How They Travel," Sutrans.org, 2006, http:// cidadanialxmob.tripod.com/shoppersandhowtheytravel.pdf.

11   City of Copenhagen statistics cited by Cycling Embassy of Denmark: http://www.cycling-embassy.dk/2013/08/26/are -cyclists-good-customers.

12   New York City Department of Transportation, "The Economic Benefits of Sustainable Streets," 2016, http://www

.nyc.gov/html/dot/downloads/pdf/dot-economic-benefits-of -sustainable-streets.pdf.

13 Donald Shoup, "Gone Parkin'," *The New York Times*, March 29, 2007.

14 Interview with the author.

15 Shoup, "Gone Parkin'."

16 Ibid.

17 Donald Shoup, "The High Cost of Minimum Parking Requirements," in *Parking: Issues and Policies (Transport and Sustainability, Volume 5)* (2014):87–113, http://shoup .bol.ucla.edu/HighCost.pdf.

18 Donald Shoup, "The High Cost of Free Parking," *Journal of Planning Education and Research*, Vol. 17 (1997):3–20, http://www.uctc.net/research/papers/351.pdf.

19 Dr. Ing Udo J. Becker, Thilo Becker, and Julia Gerlach, "The True Costs of Automobility: External Costs of Cars Overview on Existing Estimates in EU-27," October 2012, http://www.greens-efa.eu/fileadmin/dam/Documents /Studies/Costs_of_cars/The_true_costs_of_cars_EN.pdf.

20 Victoria Transport Policy Institute, "Transportation Cost and Benefit Analysis Techniques, Estimates and Implications," Updated January 2009, http://www.vtpi.org/tca.

21 Paul Tranter, "Effective Speed: Cycling Because it's 'Faster'," in Pucher and Buehler, *City Cycling,* ch. 4.

22 UK Parliament, "Memorandum from Living Streets (RS 25)," February 2008, http://www.publications.parliament.uk/pa /cm200708/cmselect/cmtran/460/460we31.htm.

23 Donald Appleyard with M. S. Gerson and M. Lintell, *Livable Streets* (Berkeley: University of California Press), 1981.

24   Joshua Hart and Prof. Graham Parkhurst, "Driven to Excess: Impacts of Motor Vehicles on the Quality of Life of Residents of Three Streets in Bristol UK," http://eprints.uwe.ac.uk /15513/1/WTPP_Hart_ParkhurstJan2011prepub.pdf.

25   Erin York Cornwell and Linda J. Waite, "Social Disconnectedness, Perceived Isolation, and Health among Older Adults," *Journal of Health and Social Behavior 2009*, Vol. 50 (March 2009):31–48, http://www.rand.org/content /dam/rand/www/external/labor/aging/rsi/rsi_papers/2009 /waite4.pdf.

26   Julianne Holt-Lunstad et al., "Loneliness and Social Isolation as Risk Factors for Mortality: A Meta-Analytic Review," *Perspectives on Psychological Science 2015*, Vol. 10(2) (2015):227–37, http://www.ahsw.org.uk/userfiles/Research /Perspectives%20on%20Psychological%20Science-2015 -Holt-Lunstad-227-37.pdf.

27   Quoted in Todd Litman, "Community Cohesion as a Transport Planning Objective," Victoria Transport Policy Institute, August 24, 2016, http://www.vtpi.org/cohesion.pdf.

28   Elizabeth Whitaker, "The Bicycle Makes the Eyes Smile: Exercise, Aging, and Psychophysical Well-Being in Older Italian Cyclists," *Medical Anthropology* 24 (2005).

CHAPTER 5

1   Interview with the author.

2   City of Seville statistics.

3   Land Transport Authority, "Passenger Transport Mode Shares in World Cities," 2011, https://www.lta.gov.sg /ltaacademy/doc/J14Nov_p54ReferenceModeShares.pdf.

4   New York City Department of Transportation, "2014 NYC In-Season Cycling Indicator," http://www.nyc.gov/html/dot /downloads/pdf/2014-isci.pdf.

5   Transport for London statistics, March 2016.

6   Transport for London statistics, June 2016.

7   Interview with the author.

8   Interview with the author.

9   Statistic from Fietsersbond.

10   Nicole Foletta, "Case Study: Houten, Utrecht, the Netherlands," ITDP Europe, 2011, https://www.itdp.org /wp-content/uploads/2014/07/22.-092211_ITDP_NED _Desktop_Houten.pdf.

11   Coroner ME Hassell, "Regulation 28: Prevention of Future Deaths Report," October 17, 2013, http://news.bbc.co.uk/2 /shared/bsp/hi/pdfs/22_10_13_cycling.pdf.

12   Peter Walker and Guy Grandjean, "A Cyclist's View of London's Notorious Cycle Superhighway 2—Video," TheGuardian.com, November 15, 2013, https://www .theguardian.com/lifeandstyle/video/2013/nov/15/cyclist -london-cycle-superhighway-2-video.

13   Transport for London, "Quietway 7 (Elephant & Castle to Crystal Palace)—Proposed changes in Lambeth–West Dulwich Area," https://consultations.tfl.gov.uk/cycling /lambeth-q7-wd.

14   Portland Bureau of Transportation, "Four Types of Transportation Cyclists," 2006, https://www.portland oregon.gov/transportation/article/158497.

15   John Forester, *Effective Cycling* (Cambridge, MA: MIT Press), 1976.

16   Interview with the author.

17   American Association of State Highway and Transportation Officials, "Guide for the Development of Bicycle Facilities," 1999, http://nacto.org/wp-content/uploads/2011/03

/AASHTO-Guide-for-the-Development-of-Bicycle-Facilities
-1999.pdf.

18   John Franklin, *Cyclecraft: The Complete Guide to Safe and
      Enjoyable Cycling for Adults and Children*, 2nd ed.
      (London: H. M. Stationery Office), 2007.

19   Interview with the author.

20   Interview with the author.

21   Interview with the author.

22   Best Conceptual Project: 2015 London Planning Awards.

23   New York City Department of Transportation, "New York
      City Cycling Risk Indicator," 2014, http://www.nyc.gov
      /html/dot/downloads/pdf/nyc-cycling-risk-indicator-2014
      .pdf.

24   Transport for London annual statistics.

25   UK Department for Transport: Reported Road Casualties,
      and National Travel Survey.

26   Peter Lyndon Jacobsen, "Safety in Numbers: More Walkers
      and Bicyclists, Safer Walking and Bicycling," *Injury
      Prevention* 9 (2003):205–9, http://www.cycle-helmets.com
      /safety_in_numbers.pdf.

27   Judy Geyer et al., "The Continuing Debate about Safety in
      Numbers—Data from Oakland, CA," Safe Transportation
      Research & Education Center. UC Berkeley, 2006, http://
      escholarship.org/uc/item/5498x882.

28   Jennifer Mindell et al., "Exposure-Based, 'Like-for-Like'
      Assessment of Road Safety by Travel Mode Using Routine
      Health Data," PLoS One, Vol. 7, 2012, http://journals.plos
      .org/plosone/article?id=10.1371/journal.pone.0050606.

29   Interview with the author.

30   Rachel Aldred, "These Deaths Are Preventable. Let's Help
      Prevent Them," RachelAldred.org, July 9, 2013, http://
      rachelaldred.org/writing/thoughts/these-deaths-are
      -preventable-lets-help-prevent-them.

CHAPTER 6

1   Interview with the author.

2   Interview with the author.

3   Dan Carrier, "CS11 Bike Route Plans: Is It Cyclists vs Tom
      Conti and the Car Drivers?" *Camden New Journal*, March 7,
      2016, http://www.camdennewjournal.com/cs11-conti.

4   UK Parliament, "Daily Hansard," Monday, December 14,
      2015, http://www.publications.parliament.uk/pa/ld201516
      /ldhansrd/text/151214-0001.htm.

5   Andrew Gilligan, " 'If You Want Cycling Improvements, You
      Have to Keep Fighting for Them,' " *The Guardian*, March 17,
      2016, https://www.theguardian.com/environment/bike-blog
      /2016/mar/17/if-you-want-cycling-improvements-you-have-
      to-keep-fighting-for-them.

6   Interview with the author.

7   Interview with the author.

8   Natalie O'Neill, "The Prospect Park West Bike Lane Had our
      Presses Rolling All Year Long," *The Brooklyn Paper*,
      December 30, 2011, http://www.brooklynpaper.com/stories
      /34/52/all_year_bikelane_2011_12_30_bk.html.

9   Interview with the author.

10   Interview with the author.

11   Odense city statistics.

12   Interview with the author.

13   "The Portland Bicycle Story," Portland State University,
      http://www.pdx.edu/ibpi/sites/www.pdx.edu.ibpi/files
      /portlandbikestory_1.pdf.

14   Michael Andersen, "Portland's New Surge in Bike Commuting
      Is Real—and It's Gas-Price Proof," BikePortland.org,
      September 5, 2016, http://bikeportland.org/2016/09/15/what
      -gas-prices-portland-bike-commuting-stays-strong-new-data
      -show-191430.

15   Odense city statistic.

16   Interview with the author.

17   Beijing Transport Research Centre (2011), cited by
      Sustainable Transport in China.

18   This is the WHO estimate; official Chinese road fatality
      statistics are widely seen as too low.

19   Interview with the author.

20   Philippines census 2015.

21   Tony Lopez, "Solving Manila's Traffic," *Manila Standard*,
      June 4, 2014, http://manilastandardtoday.com/opinion
      /columns/virtual-reality-by-tony-lopez/149020/solving
      -manila-s-traffic.html.

22   Interview with the author.

23   At *The Guardian* Live event, "How can we get more people
      cycling in London?" with author, March 10, 2016.

24   Interview with the author.

25   Interview with the author.

26   Interview with the author.

CHAPTER 7

1   Michael Polhamus, "Bill Would Require Neon Clothes, Government ID for Cyclists," *Jackson Hole News and Guide*, January 30, 2015, http://www.jhnewsandguide .com/jackson_hole_daily/local/bill-would-require-neon -clothes-government-id-for-cyclists/article_d53b9712-2e93 -517d-9e33-8f13d693ba21.html.

2   Wes Johnson, "Missouri Bill Requires Bicyclists to Fly 15-Foot Flag on Country Roads," *Springfield News-Leader*, January 14, 2016.

3   "School Pupils Encouraged to Wear Hi-Vis Vests in Road Safety Scheme," *Grimsby Telegraph*, January 23, 2012, http:// www.grimsbytelegraph.co.uk/school-pupils-encouraged-wear -hi-vis-vests-road/story-15010565-detail/story.html.

4   Chris Boardman, "Why I Didn't Wear a Helmet on BBC Breakfast," BritishCycling.org, November 3, 2014, https:// www.britishcycling.org.uk/campaigning/article/20141103 -campaigning-news-Boardman--Why-I-didn-t-wear-a -helmet-on-BBC-Breakfast-0.

5   Nick Hussey, "Why My Cycling Clothing Company Uses Models without Helmets," *The Guardian*, February 4, 2016, https://www.theguardian.com/environment/bike-blog/2016 /feb/04/vulpine-bike-clothing-company-models-without -helmets-dont-hate-us.

6   Peter Jacobsen and Harry Rutter, "Cycling Safety," in Pucher and Buehler, *City Cycling*, ch. 7.

7   "Helmets for Pedal Cyclists and for Users of Skateboards and Roller Skates," European Committee for Standardization, 1997, http://www.mrtn.ch/pdf/en_1078.pdf.

8   R.G. Attewell, K. Glase, and M. McFadden, "Bicycle Helmet Efficacy: A Meta-Analysis," *Accident Analysis and Prevention* 33 (2001).

9   Rune Elvik, "Publication bias and time-trend bias in meta-analysis of bicycle helmet efficacy: A re-analysis of Attewell, Glase and McFadden," *Accident Analysis and Prevention* 43 (2011):1245–51.

10   E-mail exchange with the author.

11   Davis, *Death on the Streets.*

12   1985 Durbin-Harvey report, commissioned by UK Department of Transport from two professors of statistics.

13   Ian Walker, "Drivers Overtaking Bicyclists: Objective Data on the Effects of Riding Position, Helmet Use, Vehicle Type and Apparent Gender," *Accident Analysis and Prevention* 39 (2007):417–25.

14   "Wearing a Helmet Puts Cyclists at Risk, Suggests Research," University of Bath, September 11, 2016, http://www.bath.ac.uk/news/articles/archive/overtaking110906.html.

15   Tim Gamble and Ian Walker, "Wearing a Bicycle Helmet Can Increase Risk Taking and Sensation Seeking in Adults," *Psychological Science*, 2016.

16   "Helmet Wearing Increases Risk Taking and Sensation Seeking," University of Bath, January 25, 2016, http://www.bath.ac.uk/news/2016/01/25/helmet-wearing-risk-taking.

17   Fishman et al., "Barriers and Facilitators to Public Bicycle Scheme Use: A Qualitative Approach," *Transportation Research Part F: Traffic Psychology and Behaviour* 15, Vol. 6 (2012):686–98.

18   Interview with the author.

19   N.C. Smith and M.W. Milthorpe, "An Observational Survey of Law Compliance and Helmet Wearing by Bicyclists in New South Wales—1993 (4th survey)." NSW Roads & Traffic Authority, 1993.

20   Colin Clarke, "Evaluation of New Zealand's Bicycle Helmet Law," *New Zealand Medical Journal* 125 (2012), http://www.cycle-helmets.com/nz-clarke-2012.pdf.

21   Chris Rissel and Li Ming Wen, "The Possible Effect on Frequency of Cycling if Mandatory Bicycle Helmet Legislation Was Repealed in Sydney, Australia: A Cross Sectional Survey," *Health Promotion Journal of Australia* 22 (2011), http://sydney.edu.au/medicine/public-health /prevention-research/pdf/HPJA_2011_Rissel.pdf.

22   Piet de Jong, "The Health Impact of Mandatory Bicycle Helmet Laws," *Risk Analysis*, 2012.

23   Beverley Turner, "It's Not Just Skiers Who Should Wear Helmets," *The Telegraph*, December 31, 2013, http://www .telegraph.co.uk/men/active/recreational-cycling/10544734 /Its-not-just-skiers-who-should-wear-helmets.html.

24   J. Carroll et al., "Jersey Scrutiny Review: Compulsory Wearing of Cycle Helmets," Transport Research Laboratory, 2014, https://www.headway.org.uk/media/3407/trl-report -compulsory-wearing-of-cycle-helmets-14-july-2014.pdf.

25   Peter Walker, "Jersey's Compulsory Cycle Helmet Law: Based on Emotion, Not Evidence?" *The Guardian*, July 30, 2014, https://www.theguardian.com/environment/bike -blog/2014/jul/30/jersey-compulsory-cycle-helmet-law -emotion-not-evidence.

26   Dorothy Robinson, "No Clear Evidence from Countries that Have Enforced the Wearing of Helmets," *British Medical Journal*, April 8, 2006.

27   Jessica Dennis et al., "Helmet Legislation and Admissions to Hospital for Cycling Related Head Injuries in Canadian Provinces and Territories: Interrupted Time Series Analysis," *British Medical Journal*, May 14, 2013.

28   Ben Goldacre and David Spiegelhalter, "Bicycle Helmets and the Law," *British Medical Journal*, June 12, 2013.

29   Shaun Helman et al., "Literature Review of Interventions to Improve the Conspicuity of Motorcyclists and Help Avoid 'Looked but Failed to See' Accidents," Transport Research Laboratory, December 13, 2012, https://msac.org.nz/assets /Uploads/pdf/Visibility-Project-TRL-Report-w.pdf.

30   Ian Walker et al., The Influence of a Bicycle Commuter's Appearance on Drivers' Overtaking Proximities: An On-Road Test of Bicyclist Stereotypes, High-visibility Clothing and Safety Aids in the United Kingdom," *Accident Analysis and Prevention* 64 (2014):69–77, http://opus.bath.ac.uk /37890/1/Walker_2013.pdf.

31   Interview with the author.

CHAPTER 8

1   Will Manners, "Scorchers v Cycle Haters: How Victorian Cyclists Were Also Vilified in the Press," *The Guardian*, October 29, 2015, https://www.theguardian.com /environment/bike-blog/2015/oct/29/scorchers-cycle-haters -how-victorian-cyclists-were-also-vilified-in-the-press.

2   Ibid.

3   Interview with the author.

4   Interview with the author.

5   "Cycling Is the New Golf," *The Economist*, April 26, 2013, http://www.economist.com/blogs/prospero/2013/04 /business-networking.

6   Helen Pidd, "Cyclists v Drivers? They're Often the Same People," *The Guardian*, August 10, 2010, https://www.the guardian.com/environment/blog/2010/aug/10/cycling-boom -survey.

7   Interview with the author.

8   "Bike-Lane Fever Grips City Officials," SILive.com, September 27, 2015, http://www.silive.com/opinion/index .ssf/2015/09/bike-lane_fever_grips_city_off.html.

9   Linda Grant, "OK, Maybe Cyclists Aren't All Bad—But the Pedestrian's Lot Is Not a Happy One Today," *The Guardian*, December 26, 2015, https://www.theguardian.com /commentisfree/2015/dec/26/ok-maybe-cyclists-arent-all-bad -but-the-pedestrians-lot-is-not-a-happy-one-today.

10   Matthew Parris, "What's Smug and Deserves to be Decapitated?" *The Times*, December 27, 2007, http://www .thetimes.co.uk/tto/opinion/columnists/matthewparris /article2044185.ece.

11   Rod Liddle, "Off Yer Bikes! Cyclists Are a Menace to Society—and Self-Righteous to Boot," *The Spectator*, November 9, 2013, http://www.spectator.co.uk/2013/11/off -your-bike.

12   "Do You Think It's Time to Ask Cyclists to Take a Test Before They're Allowed on the Roads?" (video), BBC Radio 4, May 26, 2015, http://www.bbc.co.uk/programmes/ b05vy4kk.

13   Peter Walker, "Sabotage and Hatred: What Have People Got Against Cyclists?" *The Guardian*, July 1, 2105, https://www .theguardian.com/lifeandstyle/2015/jul/01/sabotage-and -hatred-what-have-people-got-against-cyclists.

14   Carlton Reid, "Robert Goodwill Taken to Task over 'Helmet Hair' Answer," BikeBiz.com, May, 27, 2016, http://www .bikebiz.com/news/read/robert-goodwill-taken-to-task-over -helmet-hair-answer/019617.

15   Peter Walker, "When It Comes to Cycling, We're Governed by Dimwits," *The Guardian*, May 25, 2012, https://www

.theguardian.com/environment/bike-blog/2012/may/25
/cycling-governed-dimwits.

16   Interview with the author.

17   Jacob Saulwick, "Duncan Gay's Licence Plan for Cyclists
Goes Against Previous Departmental Advice," *The Sydney
Morning Herald*, July 4, 2014, http://www.smh.com.au/nsw
/duncan-gays-licence-plan-for-cyclists-goes-against-previous
-departmental-advice-20140703-zsuyi.html.

18   Interview with the author.

19   Interview with *Al-Jazeera* English, May 28, 2014.

20   Interview with the author.

21   L. Basford et al., "Drivers' Perceptions of Cyclists,"
Department for Transport, 2002, http://www.trl.co.uk
/umbraco/custom/report_files/TRL549.pdf.

22   Peter Walker, "Sabotage and Hatred: What Have People Got
Against Cyclists?" *The Guardian*, July 1, 2015, https://www
.theguardian.com/lifeandstyle/2015/jul/01/sabotage-and
-hatred-what-have-people-got-against-cyclists.

23   Ibid.

24   Marilyn Johnson et al., "Identifying Risk Factors for Cyclists
in the Australian Capital Territory," Monash University
Accident Research Centre, September 2014, http://www
.monash.edu/__data/assets/pdf_file/0019/217306/muarc322
.pdf.

25   "Hooligans," aseasyasridingabike.com, May 12, 2016,
https://aseasyasridingabike.wordpress.com/2016/05/12
/hooligans.

26   Episode broadcast January 14, 2015.

CHAPTER 9

1   Interview with the author.

2   Interview with the author.

3   Interview with the author.

4   Josh Strauss and Peter Walker, "Visijax: 'The Brightest Cycling Jacket You May Ever See'" (video), *The Guardian*, October 24, 2012, https://www.theguardian.com /environment/bike-blog/video/2012/oct/24/visijax-cycling -jacket-video.

5   Peter Walker, "The Cargo Bike—Somewhere Inbetween the Courier and the Truck," *The Guardian*, May 2, 2012, https://www.theguardian.com/environment/bike-blog/2012 /may/02/cargo-bike-city-courier-truck.

6   Ibid.

7   Interview with the author.

8   Pete Jordan, *In The City of Bikes: The Story of the Amsterdam Cyclist* (New York: Harper Perennial), 2013.

9   "Ring a Bell? It's Borrow-a-Bike Time Again . . . ," *Cambridge News*, October 12, 2007, http://www.cambridge-news.co.uk /ring-bell-borrowabike-time/story-22461332-detail/story .html.

10 Interview with the author.

11 Interview with the author.

12 Interview with the author.

13 Colin Buchanan, *Traffic in Towns: A Study of the Long Term Problems of Traffic in Urban Areas* (London: H. M. Stationery Office), 1963.

EPILOGUE

1   Carlton Reid, *Roads Were Not Built for Cars: How Cyclists Were the First to Push for Good Roads & Became the Pioneers of Motoring* (Washington, DC: Island Press), 2015.

2   Agence France-Presse, "Oslo Moves to Ban Cars from City Centre within Four Years," *The Guardian*, October 19, 2015, https://www.theguardian.com/environment/2015/oct/19/oslo-moves-to-ban-cars-from-city-centre-within-four-years.

3   "Swedish Capital to Go Car Free in September," *The Local*, July 20, 2015, http://www.thelocal.se/20150720/swedish-capital-to-go-car-free-for-a-day.

4   Adam Greenfield, "Helsinki's Ambitious Plan to Make Car Ownership Pointless in 10 Years," *The Guardian*, July 10, 2014, https://www.theguardian.com/cities/2014/jul/10/helsinki-shared-public-transport-plan-car-ownership-pointless.

5   Stephen Moss, "End of the Car Age: How Cities Are Outgrowing the Automobile," *The Guardian*, April 28, 2015, https://www.theguardian.com/cities/2015/apr/28/end-of-the-car-age-how-cities-outgrew-the-automobile.

6   Interview with the author.

7   Interview with the author.

8   Interview with the author.

9   Interview with the author.

10   Interview with the author.

ACKNOWLEDGMENTS

A lot of people helped me with this book, not least those quoted in its pages—I'm very grateful to all of them. Extra thanks to Doug Gordon, of the *Brooklyn Spoke* blog, who advised me about several people to talk to. Also thanks to Mark Wagenbuur, who runs the *Bicycle Dutch* blog and who kindly translated the Stop de Kindermoord article in chapter 2.

Finally, huge thanks to my wonderful editors, Andrew Yackira and Joanna Ng, and my fantastic agent, Rachel Mills.